Implementing Classwide PBIS

The Guilford Practical Intervention in the Schools Series

Kenneth W. Merrell, Founding Editor
Sandra M. Chafouleas, Series Editor

www.guilford.com/practical

This series presents the most reader-friendly resources available in key areas of evidence-based practice in school settings. Practitioners will find trustworthy guides on effective behavioral, mental health, and academic interventions, and assessment and measurement approaches. Covering all aspects of planning, implementing, and evaluating high-quality services for students, books in the series are carefully crafted for everyday utility. Features include ready-to-use reproducibles, lay-flat binding to facilitate photocopying, appealing visual elements, and an oversized format. Recent titles have Web pages where purchasers can download and print the reproducible materials.

Recent Volumes

School-Based Observation: A Practical Guide to Assessing Student Behavior
Amy M. Briesch, Robert J. Volpe, and Randy G. Floyd

Helping Students Overcome Social Anxiety:
Skills for Academic and Social Success (SASS)
Carrie Masia Warner, Daniela Colognori, and Chelsea Lynch

Executive Skills in Children and Adolescents, Third Edition:
A Practical Guide to Assessment and Intervention
Peg Dawson and Richard Guare

Effective Universal Instruction:
An Action-Oriented Approach to Improving Tier 1
Kimberly Gibbons, Sarah Brown, and Bradley C. Niebling

Supporting Successful Interventions in Schools:
Tools to Plan, Evaluate, and Sustain Effective Implementation
Lisa M. Hagermoser Sanetti and Melissa A. Collier-Meek

High-Impact Assessment Reports for Children and Adolescents:
A Consumer-Responsive Approach
Robert Lichtenstein and Bruce Ecker

Conducting School-Based Functional Behavioral Assessments, Third Edition:
A Practitioner's Guide
Mark W. Steege, Jamie L. Pratt, Garry Wickerd, Richard Guare, and T. Steuart Watson

Evaluating Educational Interventions, Second Edition:
Single-Case Design for Measuring Response to Intervention
T. Chris Riley-Tillman, Matthew K. Burns, and Stephen P. Kilgus

The Data-Driven School: Collaborating to Improve Student Outcomes
Daniel M. Hyson, Joseph F. Kovaleski, Benjamin Silberglitt, and Jason A. Pedersen

Implementing Classwide PBIS: A Guide to Supporting Teachers
Diane Myers, Brandi Simonsen, and Jennifer Freeman

Social and Emotional Learning in the Classroom, Second Edition:
Promoting Mental Health and Academic Success
Barbara A. Gueldner, Laura L. Feuerborn, and Kenneth W. Merrell

Implementing Classwide PBIS

A Guide to Supporting Teachers

DIANE MYERS
BRANDI SIMONSEN
JENNIFER FREEMAN

Foreword by George Sugai

THE GUILFORD PRESS
New York   London

Copyright © 2020 The Guilford Press
A Division of Guilford Publications, Inc.
370 Seventh Avenue, Suite 1200, New York, NY 10001
www.guilford.com

Printed in the United States of America

This book is printed on acid-free paper.

Last digit is print number: 9   8   7   6   5   4   3   2   1

Library of Congress Cataloging-in-Publication Data

Names: Myers, Diane, author. | Simonsen, Brandi, author. | Freeman, Jennifer, author.
Title: Implementing classwide PBIS : a guide to supporting teachers / Diane Myers,
    Brandi Simonsen, Jennifer Freeman.
Description: New York, NY : The Guilford Press, 2020. | Series: The Guilford practical
    intervention in the schools series | Includes bibliographical references and index. |
Identifiers: LCCN 2019054463 | ISBN 9781462543328 (paperback)
Subjects: LCSH: Classroom management—Psychological aspects. | School psychology. |
    Problem children—Behavior modification. | Behavior disorders in children.
Classification: LCC LB3013 .M84 2020 | DDC 371.102/4—dc23
LC record available at *https://lccn.loc.gov/2019054463*

About the Authors

Diane Myers, PhD, is Senior Vice President of Special Education for Specialized Education Services, Inc. Her prior academic appointments include serving as Professor of Special Education and Chair of the Department of Teacher Education at Texas Woman's University. Dr. Myers's research interests include implementing positive behavioral interventions and supports at the school, classroom, and individual student levels; teacher training and professional development; classroom management; and supporting students with challenging behavior. The author of numerous journal articles and book chapters, she is coauthor of *Classwide Positive Behavior Interventions and Support: A Guide to Proactive Classroom Management*.

Brandi Simonsen, PhD, is Professor in the Department of Educational Psychology and Co-Director of the Center for Behavioral Education and Research at the University of Connecticut. She is Co-Director of the Technical Assistance Center on Positive Behavior Interventions and Supports, Co-Principal Investigator of the Multi-Tiered Systems of Support Research Network, and Senior Advisor to the National Center on Intensive Intervention. Dr. Simonsen's primary interests include Tier 1 schoolwide PBIS in alternative settings, classwide PBIS, and more intensive supports for students with challenging behavior. The author of numerous journal articles and book chapters, she is coauthor of *Classwide Positive Behavior Interventions and Support: A Guide to Proactive Classroom Management*.

Jennifer Freeman, PhD, is Associate Professor in the Department of Educational Psychology and a Research Scientist at the Center for Behavioral Education and Research at the University of Connecticut. She is a recipient of the Ted Carr Initial Researcher Award from the Association for Positive Behavior Support. Dr. Freeman studies the effects of PBIS on outcomes at the high school level for high-risk student groups, including students with disabilities. She is particularly interested in improving graduation rates across and within student groups. Dr. Freeman also studies professional development methods for improving teachers' use of evidence-based classroom management strategies. She has authored numerous journal articles and book chapters.

Foreword

When the authors began writing this book, they asked if I would write a prologue (a brief narrative that comes at the beginning as an introductory preview) and an epilogue (a brief narrative that comes at the end as an overview summary) for their book. I suggested a single brief narrative that could be read at the beginning, reread at the beginning and end of each chapter, and reread again at the end of the book. They agreed.

In this foreword, I highlight why this book and each section and chapter are important, what is fundamentally the same across the book's sections and chapters, and how the book's purpose and fundamentals are important to the selection, use, and adaptation of classroom behavior management practices and systems.

My intent is to promote bridges within and across chapters and sections so that the overall contents of this book are seen as a formal system by and through which educator preparation in classroom behavior management is effective, efficient, and relevant.

Before 1980 or so, classroom behavior management was focused on the "what to do," and educators were encouraged to know and do as much as possible in the classroom, usually on their own. In addition, classroom management content was presented as "behavior" strategies and usually for students whose behaviors interfered with teaching and learning. As our knowledge and confidence have advanced (and continue to advance), our attention has expanded to the "when and how to do the what." This expansion logically shifts toward giving educators schoolwide capacity to make effective, efficient, and relevant decisions about what to do, when to do it, and how to do it with high accuracy, fluency, and durability. In addition, implementation of classroom management practices and systems is considered important preventively for *all* students and is integrated dependently into academic instruction, and vice versa.

Rather than didactically telling educators what to do and hoping that they will implement the suggestions, the authors also approach improvement of classroom behavior management practice by framing the "how and when to do" around five important implementation system features.

First, rather than reviewing an array of theoretical approaches, the authors adhere to a behavioral sciences perspective, which they describe as being empirically grounded, parsimonious in explanatory power, efficient in utilization, comprehensive in scope, and defendable as a theory. In particular, their behavioral sciences perspective (i.e., applied behavior analysis) highlights the importance and interplay of (1) human biology, (2) environmental influences, (3) observable actions and behaviors, (4) malleability and teachability of human behavior, and (5) predictable human learning and performance. As such, the context for the *what, why, when, where,* and *how* of classroom behavior management are clearly identified, described, and promoted under the umbrella of these behavioral principles.

Second, the authors have adopted the multi-tiered systems of support (MTSS) logic of the positive behavioral interventions and supports (PBIS) framework to balance the mutually informing relationships among (1) important student outcomes, (2) effective behavioral practices, (3) data-based decision making, and (4) effective and efficient implementation systems. These four elements are important, so information (*data*) is used to guide identification of and progress toward important student benefits (*outcomes*); most effective and implementable interventions (*practices*) are selected, aligned, and integrated to address these needs; and supportive professional development, training, and coaching opportunities (*systems*) are provided to educators who are responsible for implementing these practices and achieving those outcomes.

The authors extend the prevention-based continuum logic that has been applied to schoolwide PBIS to the context of effective classroom behavior management. Assessment and support of educator uses of effective classroom behavior management are streamlined using a three-tiered logic for both student and educator responsiveness. Tier 1, or universal, focuses on both what works best for supporting the learning and behavioral needs of *all* students in a classroom *and* what support systems work best for *all* educators' implementation within a school. Tier 2, or targeted, emphasizes both what additional interventions are needed for student behavior that is unresponsive to Tier 1 practices *and* what specialized support systems are needed for those educators who require more than Tier 1 professional development and implementation coaching. Finally, Tier 3, or intensive, accentuates both individualized supports for students whose behaviors are unresponsive to Tiers 1 and 2 practices *and* individualized systems for educators whose practice implementation requires more specialized professional supervision and support than offered through Tiers 1 and 2.

Third, although we always can benefit from having more empirically validated interventions in our classroom management toolboxes, the authors work from the premise that we have a great selection of effective practices and that educators must learn how to "work smarter" with the practices we know work. That is, more is not better, especially if doing more negatively affects student outcomes and our implementation accuracy and fluency over time. More important, educators must continuously monitor performance data to determine, for example, what is working, what needs to be "tweaked," and what needs to be replaced. This formative approach to practice selection, use, and impact is applied both to interventions for classroom behavior management and to systems designed for improving educator implementation integrity (i.e., accuracy, fluency, and durability).

Fourth, an important feature of the authors' approach to classroom behavior management is the application of behavioral learning theory to both student behavior and educator practice. For student learning to progress (in terms of acquisition, fluency, maintenance, and generalization), successful explicit instruction requires multiple opportunities to respond, specific corrective and positive feedback, continuous fluency-building practice, informative prompts and reminders across multiple performance environments, and a full range of learning examples. For educator practices to improve, a similar set of direct professional development practices is needed. The authors emphasize that one-time, didactic inservice professional development and preservice lecture-and-test coursework are insufficient for accurate and durable adoptions and improvements in implementation of classroom behavior management practices. As such, they focus on, for example, continuous and embedded training and practice, formal coaching supports, differentiated implementation assistance (three-tiered logic), and explicit performance feedback (corrective and acknowledging).

Finally, educators' fluent use of newly acquired skills requires training and practice; however, these experiences are insufficient. The authors emphasize that classroom behavior management must be integrated into schoolwide academic and social behavior practices and systems. As such, the establishment of common vision, language, and routine of classroom and schoolwide behavior management requires leadership structures that guide the effort—for example, (1) leadership teams coordinating and integrating implementation; (2) administrators participating in training, professional development, and daily implementation; and (3) leadership team members and administrators modeling and acknowledging language and practices that are expected from their colleagues.

I began this brief narrative by suggesting that its content serves both as an introductory overview and concluding summary of the content and themes developed by the authors. Evidence-based classroom behavior management practices are important but insufficient. The authors remind us of the importance of (1) a sound theoretical foundation, (2) a tiered continuum of support logic, (3) working smarter with a few of the most effective practices, (4) a measurable theory of learning, and (5) the vital role of leadership. These five "big themes" apply to both student and educator learning and to the content highlighted in each chapter and section.

Thus, as a user of this book, your assignment is to revisit the five implementation features of this book at the beginning, with each chapter, and at the end.

GEORGE SUGAI, PhD

Contents

Supporting Teachers' Implementation of Classwide PBIS

Foundations and Basic Principles

CHAPTER 1

Foundations of Classwide PBIS

CHAPTER OBJECTIVES

By the end of this chapter, you should be able to . . .

1. Describe classwide positive behavioral interventions and supports (CWPBIS).
2. Identify the theoretical foundations of CWPBIS.
3. Access and use other available CWPBIS resources.
4. Understand the scope and sequence of this book.

Imagine This: It is your first day as an administrator. It's the week before school begins, and you are leading your faculty through a series of professional development workshops. As you begin a session on classroom management, you see eyes roll and heads drop. "Here we go again," mutters one teacher in the back row. "Let's see what this year's gimmick will be," says another. Disheartened, you review your remarks and realize that the 2-hour workshop you planned will in no way begin to address the school's excessive discipline referrals, teacher morale, and lack of systematic behavior support for all students. "OK," you say, addressing the group, "Let's look at some data, and let's talk about a systematic, evidence-based framework for delivering behavior support in the classroom."

THE RESEARCH-TO-PRACTICE GAP IN CLASSROOM MANAGEMENT

Classroom management can be a challenge for even the most skilled teacher. Each year, students arrive with a range of behavioral needs, and teachers may not always have the repertoire of practices needed to best support everyone in their classrooms. Many teachers report feeling unprepared to deal with students' difficult behaviors (e.g., Freeman, Simonsen, Briere, & MacSuga-Gage, 2014; Oliver & Reschly, 2007, 2010). The responsibility for ensuring that teachers are well prepared to support all students' behavior falls on teacher preparation programs (e.g., colleges and universities with teacher education programs, alternative route to certification programs) and providers of professional development, but evidence indicates that we are not doing enough (e.g., Landers, Alter, & Servilio, 2008; Myers, Freeman, Simonsen, & Sugai, 2017). The United States has a high turnover rate among teachers, which is due at least in part to teachers' struggles with classroom management (Klassen & Chiu, 2010; Landers et al., 2008). In order to attract teachers to the field and to keep them in the classroom, we need to ensure that they have the skills and support they need to be effective classroom managers.

The good news is this: We know what works (i.e., the **research** piece). Several decades of research have provided evidence about practices that will positively impact students' (and teachers') behavior in the classroom (Office of Special Education Programs [OSEP], 2015; Simonsen, Fairbanks, Briesch, Myers, & Sugai, 2008; Simonsen & Myers, 2015). We discuss some of these empirically supported practices and provide additional resources in upcoming sections of this chapter. Despite knowing what works, though, teachers often do not implement these empirically supported practices with the frequency and fidelity that leads to improved student behavior (e.g., Forman, Olin, Eaton Hoagwood, Crowe, & Saka, 2009; Myers, Sugai, Simonsen, & Freeman, 2017; Reinke, Herman, Stormont, Newcomer, & David, 2013). This **practice** piece can be a challenge: How can we support teachers' implementation of and fluency with empirically supported practices in classroom management? We hope this book will help to answer that question.

THEORETICAL FOUNDATIONS OF CWPBIS

Let's begin with a very quick look at the theoretical underpinnings of our approach to classroom management. We apply a positive behavioral interventions and supports (i.e., PBIS) framework at the classwide level (i.e., CWPBIS). PBIS is heavily influenced by behaviorism and an applied, scientific approach to human behavior (i.e., applied behavior analysis [ABA]) (Alberto & Troutman, 2016; Cooper, Heron, & Heward, 2007). In a behavioral approach, the interventionist (who, in CWPBIS, is usually the teacher) explores the impact of the environment on an individual's behavior and makes changes to the environment to increase or decrease the likelihood of certain behaviors. Elements of the classroom environment that can be changed include the arrangement of the classroom, the distribution of rewards contingent on appropriate behavior, and the teacher's own behavior. If a teacher can understand which environmental conditions increase the likelihood of appropriate student behavior, he or she can provide those conditions. For example, if third-grade teacher Mr. Sanchez observes that his students are more on task when the window shades are down, he can lower the shades to increase the likelihood of on-task behavior. Similarly, if high school science teacher Ms. Langston notices that her students are more likely to participate when she gives specific praise related to participation (e.g., "I like how you raised your hand, Simone.

What did you want to contribute?"), she can provide more specific praise statements when she wants to increase participation.

A full description of the science of behavior is beyond the scope of this chapter. We address many behavioral principles in Chapter 2, including descriptions and applied examples of key concepts such as antecedents, consequences, and stimulus control. In the meantime, for a more in-depth explanation of an applied science of behavior, we suggest the following resources: *Applied Behavior Analysis for Teachers* (9th edition), by Paul Alberto and Anne Troutman; *Applied Behavior Analysis* (2nd edition), by John Cooper, Timothy Heron, and William Heward; and *Classwide Positive Behavior Interventions and Supports: A Guide to Proactive Classroom Management* (especially Chapter 1), by Brandi Simonsen and Diane Myers (yes, two of the authors of this book!). (Full reference information for these resources and all others mentioned is available in the "References" section at the back of this book.) Without a fundamental understanding of how behavior works, teachers may struggle to make the connection between theory and practice; that is, they will not understand why what they are doing has (or does not have) an impact on student behavior.

PBIS began as a user-friendly way to deliver individual, empirically supported, ABA-based behavioral supports to people with behavioral needs (e.g., Carr et al., 2002). Researchers and practitioners realized the potential that a PBIS approach could have at the school-wide level and began developing a schoolwide PBIS framework (i.e., SWPBIS; Turnbull et al., 2002). SWPBIS is a multi-tiered system of support (MTSS) based on the public health model (Walker et al., 1996). In this model, all members of a population (in a school, those members include students, faculty, staff, and administration) receive a universal level of preventative support. We often call this initial level of support "Tier 1." In SWPBIS, these supports include establishing agreed-upon expectations (e.g., "be safe," "be responsible," "be respectful"), teaching those expectations to all students in the context of routines (e.g., hallway, cafeteria, bus), developing a system for responding to student behavior that meets expectations, and consistently collecting data that are then used to evaluate SWPBIS in context and make modifications as necessary. Visit the OSEP PBIS Technical Assistance Center (*www.pbis.org*) for resources, research, and other information related to PBIS.

Outcomes, Data, Systems, and Practices

PBIS has four core elements: *outcomes*, *data*, *systems*, and *practices* (Sugai et al., 2010). The chapters in this book explore each of these elements as they relate to the content being presented, so it makes sense to introduce them briefly here. First, implementing any PBIS framework—be it at the schoolwide, classwide, or teacher-training level—requires **outcomes**. That is, what is it that you hope to achieve by adopting PBIS? We have found that teachers, administrators, and other education personnel generally agree on two overarching outcomes: improved student behavior and improved academic performance. Once stakeholders (e.g., PBIS team members, school faculty, others with a vested interest) have agreed on outcomes, they must agree on how to measure those outcomes, which involves the collection and evaluation of relevant **data**. For example, if a classroom teacher is interested in "increased student participation" as an outcome, he could track the number of hand-raises during a discussion and see whether that number increases after implementing a specific **practice** (e.g., token economy). **Practices** are those interventions and strategies that we implement in order to achieve our outcomes; these are what will ultimately increase or decrease the likelihood of specific behaviors and should be selected based on available evidence of their efficacy and contextual and cultural appropriateness. (A discussion of empirically supported classroom management practices follows in the next section of this chapter.)

Finally, the success and sustainability of any PBIS effort depends on the **systems** that support PBIS implementation and maintenance. These systems include a plan for training (e.g., teaching students about the expectations, teaching faculty members to use CWPBIS practices) that is ongoing; one brief overview will not result in long-term effects. In addition to training, a functional PBIS model will have a system for data collection and evaluation, a system for responding to appropriate behavior, and a system for responding to inappropriate behavior. We often refer to the systems piece as the "heart" of any PBIS model; without systems, PBIS would not be able to sustain itself. If you would like a more in-depth explanation and discussion of these core elements of PBIS, refer to Sugai and colleagues (2010) and Simonsen and Myers (2015; especially Chapter 3).

EMPIRICALLY SUPPORTED PRACTICES IN CLASSROOM MANAGEMENT

Earlier, we said that we know what works, so let's start with an overview of effective classroom management practices that we'd like to see all teachers using in the classroom. We use the term "empirically supported" to describe practices that have substantial, rigorous evidence demonstrating their effectiveness. These practices have been (1) implemented and evaluated by researchers, (2) associated with measurable and documented effects on students' behavior, and (3) able to demonstrate efficacy across settings. Below, we organize our brief discussion of these empirically supported classroom management practices in broad categories (i.e., maximizing structure and actively engaging students during instruction; establishing and teaching positively stated expectations; implementing a continuum of strategies to reinforce appropriate behavior; and implementing a continuum of strategies to respond to inappropriate behavior) and provide specific examples of the practices within each category.

MAXIMIZING STRUCTURE AND ACTIVELY ENGAGING STUDENTS DURING INSTRUCTION

Structure in a classroom comprises several elements over which teachers exert a major influence (for the most part; certainly, there are some structural aspects—e.g., placement of doors and windows—that are beyond the teacher's control). First, there is the visible physical structure of the classroom (e.g., where furniture is placed, wall decor). Second, there is the organizational structure of the classroom (e.g., rules and expectations, reward system). Finally, there is the instructional structure of the classroom (e.g., how lessons are delivered, planned student engagement). A few key practices to maximize structure and actively engage students during instruction are outlined next; for a comprehensive look at CWPBIS practices, refer to Simonsen and Myers (2015).

Establishing and Teaching Classroom Routines

Establishing and teaching classroom routines is a critical part of the embedded structure in the classroom. Both students and teachers need to be fluent with when and how routines are executed. All day-to-day operations in the classroom should have established routines that have been specifically taught to students, including how to ask for help, procedures for using the restroom, where to find missed assignments due to absences, what to do if they are finished with a quiz before other students—the list goes on and on. Each classroom will have a unique set of routines that are contextually appropriate; that is, the routines are developed with consideration of students' ages, ability levels, and background knowledge. For example, in a kindergarten class, Miss Cruise may teach her students exactly what it looks like to sit appropriately during circle time (i.e., the circle time routine): legs crossed, eyes on teacher, hands and feet to self. This would not be appropriate for Mr. Perry's high school history class; instead, he may teach students exactly what it looks like to participate appropriately in a class debate (i.e., the debate routine): hand raised to participate, waiting for others to finish before speaking, ending comments when prompted by the timer or the moderator. Teaching classroom expectations will be addressed in a subsequent section.

Arranging the Classroom Environment to Promote Appropriate Behavior

All classrooms are different, and there is not a single way to arrange the classroom that will guarantee improved student behavior. What we do recommend is that the classroom be arranged to minimize crowding and distraction. All decor should be relevant and enhance students' ability to attend to instruction, rather than detract from it. Teachers should arrange the room so that they can adequately supervise all students; each student should be able to see the teacher, and the teacher (and students) should be able to move around freely without obstructions or furniture blocking traffic flow. This attention to arrangement will also help with transitions. Transition routines should be taught and practiced, as transitions are times when students may be more likely to engage in behavior that does not meet expectations. When planning the arrangement of the classroom, teachers should always be focused on the instructional approach and outcomes. If a lesson is group-based, the desks should be in clusters. If independent work is the goal, rows may be more appropriate. If a teacher wants to focus on academic talk and improved social skills between students, paired desks may make the most sense.

Actively Engaging Students in Instruction

Do you know a teacher who has never had any formal training in classroom management, yet he or she rarely has classroom management issues? There's a good chance that teacher is a pro at engaging students in instruction. Students who are actively engaged in instruction are much less likely to be involved in inappropriate behavior—those are two mutually exclusive responses! Teachers can use a variety of empirically supported practices to engage students in instruction, including high rates and varied styles of opportunities to respond (OTRs). OTRs could be as simple as asking students an academic question (e.g., "Who knows the capital of Manitoba?") or as complex as asking for a written explanation of the impact of the Treaty of Versailles on the end of World War I. OTRs can be gestural (e.g., "Give me a thumbs up if you agree that the answer is 42"); they can be individual ("Sammy, show me where the page number is located") or done in unison ("Class, on my count, everyone tell me the name of our president"). To be a true "opportunity" for students, the students must have the capacity to respond; that is, the OTR must be developmentally, contextually, and academically appropriate. High rates of OTRs are associated with increased student engagement (Simonsen et al., 2008), and increased student engagement generally results in increased academic performance—one of those overarching goals that all educators desire. In addition to OTRs, other practices associated with increased student engagement include direct, explicit instruction, classwide peer tutoring, computer-assisted instruction, and guided notes (Simonsen & Myers, 2015).

Maximizing structure affects the **antecedents** that occasion (i.e., "signal" the availability of reinforcement for) behaviors. We discuss antecedents and antecedent control much more in upcoming chapters. Antecedents alone do not increase or decrease the likelihood of behaviors that meet classroom expectations, but thoughtful consideration of environmental stimuli (e.g., furniture placement, visible rules) and other structural aspects of the classroom can increase the likelihood that students (and teachers) will know and perform desired behaviors at the appropriate times.

ESTABLISHING AND TEACHING POSITIVELY STATED EXPECTATIONS

In addition to maximizing both the physical and embedded structures in the classroom, teachers should establish and teach their classroom expectations to students (just as teachers would teach academic content that they wanted students to know and be able to apply). In a CWPBIS model, a teacher chooses between three and five positively stated expectations for the classroom (Simonsen & Myers, 2015). These expectations should be broad (e.g., "be respectful") so they can be defined across a variety of routines. These expectations should be positively stated for several reasons. First, we want to remind students of what they *should* be doing rather than what they *should not* be doing. For example, if someone tells you "Don't run," you instantly think of running—which is *not* the desired behavior. It's much more effective to say "Walk," which reminds the learner only of the desired behavior.

Positively stated expectations also create a more positive classroom environment, which is challenging if teachers only have a list of "no, stop, don't" rules. Finally, if teachers have a list of "no, stop, don't" rules, students will inevitably find behaviors that are not explicitly prohibited in the classroom and promptly engage in them. (Imagine the list a teacher would need to have in order to discourage every possible problem behavior!) If teachers are in a school where SWPBIS is already in place, then the schoolwide expectations can be used as classroom expectations, which will help enhance consistency in language and behavior between environments.

Once a teacher has established a small number of positively stated general expectations, he or she needs to define these expectations in the context of classroom routines. We mentioned classroom routines in the previous section. These routines provide the embedded structure of the classroom and are critical to an efficient, effective learning environment. Teachers cannot assume that students will know how to execute behaviors that meet expectations; for example, students may have very different ideas of what "being respectful" looks like (if "be respectful" is one of the classroom expectations). Teachers should select a reasonable number of classroom routines (we suggest no more than five to seven) and define their expectations in the context of those routines. For example, if one of the expectations is "be responsible" and one of the routines is "independent seat work," the following behaviors specifically define what that expectation looks like within that routine: "Keep your eyes on your own work," "Place completed work in the bin on the teacher's desk," and "Read all directions before beginning your work." One of the easiest ways to organize these defined behaviors is to create an expectations-within-routines matrix (see Figure 1.1 for an example).

After desired behaviors have been explicitly defined, teachers need to develop a plan for teaching those behaviors to their students. Teachers should identify a scope and sequence of instruction appropriate for their students' ages and ability levels (e.g., When will lessons be taught? How often will social behavior lessons be taught? How will they be categorized—by expectation, by routine, or in another manner?). After the timeline is determined, teachers should systematically (there's that "systems" piece of PBIS!) roll out instruction of the classroom expectations by explicitly teaching them to students in the same manner in which academic content is taught. That is, lessons should be specific; they should have measurable outcomes and a system for evaluating those outcomes; and they should follow a direct instructional approach (i.e., using a model–lead–test format, or "I do," "We do," "You do"). As with academic lessons, teachers should collect data to determine the effectiveness of expectation-related instruction and use those data to guide teaching (or reteach, if necessary).

Establishing positively stated expectations for the classroom ensures that all students (and teachers) will know exactly what behaviors are expected and when to execute those behaviors. Just as with academic content, expectations need to be taught explicitly, with meaningful instructional activities and informative assessment. In addition, students will need periodic reminders about the expectations. We know that students sometimes will forget academic content (what is the capital of Manitoba, anyway?) and may need review sessions or booster trainings; this same principle holds true for social behavior content as well.

	Arrival	Dismissal	Group Activities	Whole-Class Instruction	Independent Seatwork
Organized	Put everything in locker neatly. Turn your phone off and put it away.	Pack up all materials at your desk after the bell rings. Walk single-file to your locker.	Review who is assigned which role in the group. Review directions before beginning.	Have only what you need for class on your desk. Take helpful notes.	Have all needed materials on desk or nearby. Sharpen pencil before beginning tasks.
Prepared	Have all materials you need for the day. Have your student ID visible.	Write down all homework assignments. Bring home needed materials.	Follow all directions for group work. Complete all of your assigned tasks.	Complete all assigned readings prior to class. Write down details about assignments.	Be sure any needed technology is charged. Review directions prior to beginning.
Enthusiastic	Put homework in the correct bin. Begin the "do now" as soon as you sit down.	Select one thing you learned today to share with your family and write it down in your planner.	Introduce yourself to all group members. Set goals about timeline and productivity.	Actively contribute to class discussions. Look up related resources on the Internet after class.	Stay on task with phone off and away. Take notes on questions for teacher after class.
Nice	Greet your peers and your teacher. Hold the door for others who are entering.	Say good-bye to your peers and your teacher. Hold the door for people behind you.	Actively listen to other group members. Offer to help any group members who are struggling.	Raise hand to participate. If partnering, select someone different each time.	Raise hand if you have a question. Keep silent while working.

FIGURE 1.1. Example of rules-within-routine matrix for a seventh-grade classroom in an SWPBIS school in which all students are encouraged to "Be OPEN-minded."

IMPLEMENTING A CONTINUUM OF STRATEGIES TO REINFORCE APPROPRIATE BEHAVIOR

As we discuss in the following chapters, it is the **consequences** of a behavior that will actually increase, maintain, or decrease the likelihood of a behavior in the future. That is, behaviors followed by pleasant consequences to the learner tend to be repeated, and behaviors followed by unpleasant consequences to the learner tend not to be repeated. If teachers go through the efforts to maximize structure, actively engage students, establish expectations, and then explicitly teach those expectations to students, teachers should make sure to provide consequences that are likely to increase students' desired behaviors and make all of that careful preparation worthwhile. There are several empirically supported practices that teachers can use to increase the likelihood of behavior that meets expectations, including behavior-specific praise, group contingencies, behavior contracting, and token economies (Simonsen & Myers, 2015). We take a closer look at these next.

Behavior-Specific Praise

Praise is a common social reinforcer used frequently by teachers. The most effective kind of praise is specific (i.e., the behavior being praised is explicitly stated) and contingent (i.e., it directly follows the behavior so the relationship between the behavior and the praise statement is clear to the learner). Specific praise statements have been associated with increases in appropriate student behavior across multiple populations (Simonsen et al., 2008) and are one of the most efficient and effective practices that teachers can employ in their CWPBIS systems. In fact, we consider it non-negotiable; that is, all teachers should be implementing specific praise in their classrooms without exception. Here are some examples of behavior-specific praise statements:

- "Brandi, you've done a great job completing this assignment neatly. That's what it looks like to work responsibly."
- "Jen, thank you for helping Teddy pick up his area and showing good citizenship."
- "George, I like how you raised your hand to participate."

Behavior-specific praise statements are intended to reinforce (i.e., increase the future likelihood of) behavior that meets expectations, but they serve other purposes, too. A behavior-specific praise statement is a verbal **prompt** (see a full description of prompting in upcoming chapters) for all students about expected behaviors; that is, when Diane hears George being praised for raising his hand, she is reminded that hand raising is a desired behavior. In addition, teachers can only deliver behavior-specific praise if they are paying attention to students' behavior. For students who find attention reinforcing, specific praise statements can provide attention contingent on an appropriate behavior. At a minimum, all teachers should be using behavior-specific praise to reinforce appropriate behavior, but there are other practices on the continuum that teachers may decide to incorporate into a CWPBIS system.

Group Contingencies

Group contingencies have been associated with increases in appropriate behavior (Alberto & Troutman, 2016). In a group contingency, all learners in a group must perform the target behavior to earn the same reward. There are three types of group contingencies:

1. In a **dependent** group contingency, one or a few learners perform a behavior and everyone receives a reward. For example, "When Lisa and Tim turn in 10 homework assignments each, the class earns an extra recess."
2. In an **interdependent** group contingency, each learner in the group must perform the target behavior in order for the group to receive the reward. For example, "When everyone has read at least three books, we will have a pizza party."
3. In an **independent** group contingency, whether or not the learner receives the reward depends entirely on his or her own performance of the desired behavior. For example, "If you clean up your area after art class, you can have 5 minutes of free time."

Teachers may use variations of the group contingency (e.g., a marble jar wherein a teacher places a marble each time she "catches" someone behaving appropriately; when there are a certain number of marbles, the class earns a movie or other reward). There are several caveats for using group contingencies, and we urge teachers to only use group contingencies if the possible benefits, possible risks, and systematic implementation have been carefully considered. In the dependent and interdependent group contingencies, there is the risk of peer pressure. Teachers can mitigate this risk by promoting the contingency as an opportunity for community building and teaching students (using specific instruction, as described above) what it looks like to encourage and support one another. In the dependent group contingency, students who do not perform the desired behavior (or who engage in other inappropriate behaviors) may still earn the reward if the contingency is not set up carefully. In any of the group contingencies, learners may be less likely to perform the desired behavior if the reward is not reinforcing to them. For example, what if learners don't like recess? Or pizza? These students may not be motivated to do their part (either by performing the desired behavior or by encouraging classmates) to earn that reward, thus threatening the success of the group contingency as an effective strategy for increasing appropriate behavior. Luckily, we have other options.

Behavioral Contracting

Although many teachers consider behavioral contracts to be an option for students who are struggling to meet behavioral expectations, we urge teachers to think about behavioral contracts as a way to proactively encourage appropriate behavior. Behavioral contracts can be used in conjunction with other reinforcement strategies (e.g., token economy) and mimic contracts found in the real world because they (1) are documented, (2) contain terms that were negotiated by both parties, (3) state what will happen if certain behaviors are completed (and if they are not completed), and (4) are reviewed regularly to ensure compliance (Alberto & Troutman, 2016; Simonsen & Myers, 2015). Behavioral contracts must be fair, contain specific details about the expected behaviors, and state how, what, and when rewards will be delivered.

Behavioral contracts should focus on the desired behaviors rather than the absence of inappropriate behaviors. For example, if a student was working on his time on task, one expectation in the contract could read, "If Dante remains on task (i.e., following directions, oriented toward teacher during lesson, oriented toward work during desk work, observing all classroom rules) for 20 out of 30 minutes during a given English class, he will earn 5 minutes of iPad time to be redeemed at the end of the day." In addition, contracts can specify additional contingencies if the student exceeds expectations: "If Dante remains on task for all 30 minutes of a given English class, he will earn 15 minutes of iPad time to be redeemed at the end of the day."

Token Economies

Most teachers have some familiarity with token economies, and we encourage all teachers to use this widely researched practice in their classrooms as a way to support and reinforce appropriate student behavior (Simonsen & Myers, 2015). Token economies are an overt system for recognizing and rewarding target behaviors, and although they may vary widely in appearance and delivery, all token economies should have the following components:

- **Tokens**, which are delivered contingently on the appropriate behavior. These can be tickets, stickers, points, play coins, or anything that can be easily delivered and counted (as they will be exchanged for backup reinforcers).
- **Backup reinforcers**, which should offer students a variety of reward options. Teachers may create a "menu" of backup reinforcers that could be activity based (e.g., 10 minutes iPad time), tangible (e.g., pencil or pen), or social (e.g., lunch with a friend).
- An **exchange system** that clearly outlines both the exchange rate, that is, the "cost" (in tokens) of each backup reinforcer, and the process for exchange (i.e., when and where exchanges take place).

Unlike group contingencies, token economies offer students different rewards for the same behaviors, thereby increasing the likelihood that students will be reinforced for the appropriate behavior and more likely to engage in that behavior in the future. Also, tokens can be delivered discreetly and can bear a quantitative relationship to the behavior being performed (unlike specific praise, which is usually verbal and does not vary in quantity as tokens can). For instance, "Great job raising your hand!" and "Great job helping Stanley pick up his books!" (after another student knocked them out of Stanley's hands) provide the same amount of reinforcement for both behaviors, one of which clearly requires more effort. In a token economy, hand raising could be a "one-token" behavior and helping another in a situation like that could be considered a "ten-token" behavior.

Token economies do require more planning and consistent evaluation than other prac-tices, but token economies can have an enormous payoff in terms of improved student behavior, making the effort well worth it. In addition, token economies mimic the monetary economy in which we all live (i.e., we earn a salary or wages for performing a task, and we exchange that payment for items that we need or want) and can be a valuable learning tool for students if the token economy is monitored regularly and tweaked as needed (according to behavioral data and level of support required) and culturally appropriate for the ages and context of the classroom.

IMPLEMENTING A CONTINUUM OF STRATEGIES TO RESPOND TO INAPPROPRIATE BEHAVIOR

Even in classrooms where teachers apply all of the strategies described above, collect data regularly, and use those data to make effective instructional decisions, there will still be student behaviors that do not meet expectations. When this happens, teachers should have a continuum of strategies to respond to students' inappropriate behaviors. We have outlined several of these strategies below. For more detailed information, see Alberto and Troutman (2016) or Simonsen and Myers (2015). (Also, the resources mentioned in the "Suggested Resources" section toward the end of this chapter provide much more in-depth information on all theories, practices, and systems discussed in this chapter.)

Behavior-Specific Error Correction

The first response to a low-level behavioral error should be similar to a teacher's response to an academic error. When a student makes an error when reading aloud (e.g., she says "through" when the word is "thorough"), the teacher will usually respond by pointing out that an error was made (e.g., "Can you try that again?"), helping to correct the error as needed (e.g., "Be sure to read the word completely"), providing increasing levels of prompts if necessary (e.g., "Read it with me: *thorough*"), and giving contingent positive feedback if the student corrects the error (e.g., "That's right. Keep reading!"). Teachers usually do not follow this instructional, helpful approach when responding to social behavioral errors. If a student calls out instead of raising her hand, common teacher responses include, "Stop calling out," "Don't be disruptive," or similar types of reprimands. Behavior-specific error correction looks different:

STUDENT: (*without raising hand*) Miss Newman! Miss Newman! I know!

MISS NEWMAN: Shawn, remember what it looks like to be responsible when participat-ing in class? Calling out is not being responsible. Show me what being responsible looks like.

STUDENT: (*Raises hand.*)

MISS NEWMAN: Great job raising your hand, Shawn. Now, what is your answer?

Rather than just issuing a reprimand that does not remind Shawn of the desired behavior, Miss Newman points out the error, reminds the student of the desired behavior, gives him an opportunity to engage in the desired behavior, and acknowledges when the desired behavior occurs. As with academic behaviors, students will only learn social behaviors with practice and feedback. Of course, not all behaviors are low-level enough to warrant this kind of response (e.g., behavior-specific error correction would be an inappropriate teacher response to a fistfight in the classroom), and not all student behaviors will respond to this strategy. Behavior-specific error correction is one response in our continuum of strategies, and all teachers should be able to apply this strategy in their classrooms when appropriate.

Other Responses to Inappropriate Behavior

There are other strategies that can decrease the likelihood of inappropriate student behavior. A complete discussion of them is beyond the scope of this chapter, but we look briefly at several of them next.

Differential Reinforcement

Differential reinforcement is a strategy usually applied at the individual-student (rather than whole-class) level. There are different types of differential reinforcement, all of which apply a special schedule of reinforcement to decrease the frequency of inappropriate behaviors and increase the frequency of appropriate behaviors. These specific schedules of differential reinforcement (DR) include the following:

- **Differential reinforcement of lower rates of behavior (DRL)**, which reinforces a lower level of a target behavior that is inappropriate primarily due to its frequency. For example, asking to get a drink is an acceptable behavior when the frequency is low, but it is unacceptable when it happens too often. A teacher may use DRL as follows: "Sam, asking to get a drink is fine once in a while, but asking three or four times an hour is not fine. If you can limit yourself to asking for just one drink before lunch and one drink after, you can be the line leader this afternoon."

- **Differential reinforcement of other behaviors (DRO)**, which reinforces an absence of the target behavior after a certain period of time. A teacher may use DRO as follows: "Santiago, if you can refrain from talking to Sarah for the next 20 minutes of class, you can have 5 minutes to converse at the end of the period." (The teacher will need to ensure that Santiago is being reinforced for remaining quiet and on task and that any other inappropriate behaviors—such as writing notes to Sarah or making kissing noises, neither of which is "talking"—will nullify the delivery of the reinforcement.)

- **Differential reinforcement of alternative behaviors (DRA)**, which—happily—teachers should be doing already if they are following a CWPBIS model. With DRA, teachers reinforce a socially acceptable behavior that is an alternative to the target behavior. For instance, for a student who struggles to keep his hands to himself, a teacher may reinforce an alternative behavior whenever possible: "Simon, I like how you have your hands in your pockets," or "John, thank you for keeping your hands at your sides/your feet on the floor."

Differential reinforcement can increase the focus on appropriate behavior and decrease the likelihood of inappropriate behaviors, especially when paired with other strategies for increasing appropriate behavior (e.g., behavior-specific praise, token economies). In any PBIS model, we want to avoid introducing aversive stimuli into the environment as a primary response to inappropriate behavior and instead use an instructional, proactive, and positive approach to increasing those behaviors that we do want to see in the classroom.

One term sometimes used when discussing behavior management in the classroom is **noncontingent reinforcement**. Although this term can be confusing (because, after all, reinforcement is delivered contingently on a behavior), we want you to be familiar with it in case you hear it being used in the field. In noncontingent reinforcement, reinforcers are delivered regardless of a student's behavior (Alberto & Troutman, 2016). For example, if a student's off-task behavior is being maintained by peer attention, the teacher may schedule "chat breaks" or similar things that are not contingent on appropriate behavior but that provide the desired peer attention. Noncontingent reinforcement may be used in conjunction with DRA.

Planned Ignoring

When students' inappropriate behavior functions to obtain attention, it can be difficult for teachers to respond to the behavior *without* providing attention. For instance, if a student is calling out the teacher's name loudly, in a singsong manner, and repeatedly (in other words, the student is not meeting expectations), the teacher is likely to respond with a look and probably a reprimand or error correction—all of which provides contingent attention (which the student likely finds reinforcing) that will maintain or increase the likelihood of that behavior in the future. For inappropriate behaviors that function to gain attention, teachers can use **planned ignoring** to decrease the likelihood of those attention-seeking behaviors. This means that when a student is engaging in an inappropriate behavior to get attention, the teacher must plan to ignore the behavior (i.e., not provide any contingent attention). Before using planned ignoring, the teacher must make sure that the student has ample instruction in, and opportunity to practice, the desired replacement behavior (e.g., raising a hand, in our example of the student who calls out inappropriately). The teacher should provide as much contingent attention as possible for the appropriate behavior; in addition, teachers should prompt often for the desired behavior (e.g., prior to a class discussion, the teacher says to the student, "Michael, remember to raise your hand if you want my attention"). If a teacher is using planned ignoring, he or she must withhold all attention (i.e., looks, gestures, comments) to ensure that the inappropriate behavior is not being reinforced, and the teacher must be prepared for the possibility that the behavior will intensify before it begins to decrease. After all, the student is used to being reinforced for a certain behavior, so when there is no reinforcement, the student may simply try again, and increase the intensity of the behavior to better the chances of reinforcement. (Think about a child in the grocery store who is told "No" when she asks for candy. If the child is used to getting candy, she's very likely to ask—or demand—again, and the situation can escalate quickly!) Planned ignoring should be used judiciously and only in conjunction with teaching, prompting, and reinforcing of the desired behaviors.

Overcorrection

Teachers may consider using **overcorrection** to decrease the future likelihood of inappropriate behavior. Overcorrection requires the learner to engage in an exaggerated or extended practice of an appropriate behavior contingent on a related inappropriate behavior (Alberto & Troutman, 2016). For example, if a student vandalizes a stall in the restroom, the teacher may have the student clean off his graffiti (simple correction) and then have the student clean off the other graffiti in the other stalls (overcorrection). Specifically, that is an example of **restitutional overcorrection**, when a student "makes restitution" (and then some) for an inappropriate behavior. Here's another example: Several students run while lining up for lunch. The teacher has the students walk back to their seats and line up according to expectations (i.e., hands at sides, walking) and then has them repeat lining up appropriately five more times, which would be considered **positive practice overcorrection**. We sometimes see this concept applied in academics—for example, students may write a misspelled word several times to practice the correct spelling. While we don't want students associating an appropriate behavior with an aversive consequence, overcorrection can be helpful in reducing future inappropriate behaviors while providing students extended practice of an appropriate behavior and increasing students' sense of accountability for their actions.

Time-Out from Reinforcement

Sometimes, a time-out from reinforcement may be an effective strategy for decreasing the likelihood of future inappropriate behaviors. Note that in order for this strategy to work, the time-out must actually be from an activity or setting that the student finds reinforcing. Removing a student from an environment (contingent on misbehavior) in which the student didn't want to be only reinforces the misbehavior by providing the student a chance to get away. The next time the student doesn't want to be there, he or she is likely to engage in the same misbehavior that resulted in escape the last time. One appropriate application of time-out from reinforcement could occur when a student who is enjoying recess is being rowdier than allowed at recess and is removed (i.e., told to sit and watch) for a specific amount of time. Also, in a classroom, if a student is telling jokes to his delighted group members, the student may be asked to work alone for 15 minutes before being able to return to the group. Using time-out effectively can be challenging for teachers, and we recommend its use only (1) as one possible strategy on a continuum of responses to inappropriate behavior that is embedded in a comprehensive CWPBIS system and (2) when combined with practices to teach and reinforce expectation-following behaviors.

THE PHASES OF LEARNING

As we've discussed in the previous sections, an effective CWPBIS model requires foundational knowledge about behavior, skilled implementation of empirically supported practices, the ability to sustain those practices over time, and the ability to continue implementation—with tweaks, as needed—across populations of diverse ability levels, backgrounds, cultures, and ages. We believe that learning classroom management is like learning most other skill sets, and we frame that in the *phases of learning model* (Alberto & Troutman, 2016; Cooper et al., 2007; Simonsen & Myers, 2015). The phases of learning (acquisition, fluency, maintenance, and generalization) lead sequentially to the end goal of a learner being able to apply what he or she has learned across settings and time. We use this model to guide our own instruction, and we use it to frame this book, as well. The phases are described briefly below (see Figure 1.2 for a visual depiction of the phases).

Acquisition

In the **acquisition** phase, a learner is exposed to new content. During this phase, the focus is on acquiring knowledge to be able to formulate accurate behavioral responses. Teachers should expect mistakes during the acquisition phase and be ready to provide specific feedback to support students' acquisition of new knowledge. Think of first graders learning to read, high school students learning to factor equations, or adults learning new technology for the first time. There will be errors, but eventually the learners should build a solid base of knowledge related to the new concept.

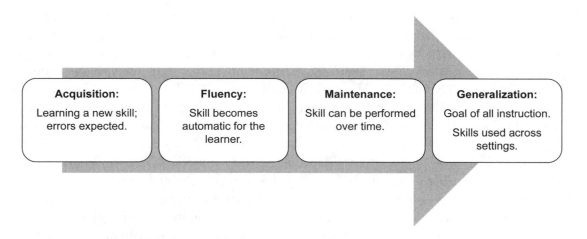

Acquisition:
Learning a new skill; errors expected.

Fluency:
Skill becomes automatic for the learner.

Maintenance:
Skill can be performed over time.

Generalization:
Goal of all instruction.

Skills used across settings.

FIGURE 1.2. Visual representation of the phases of learning.

During the **fluency** phase, the focus is on the rate of responding. Learners should be able to execute the new behavior in a way that makes the behavior functional. If a student must sound out each letter when reading, he is not yet in the fluency phase of learning, and reading is not yet a functional skill for that student. If an adult still has to read the instructional manual each time she wants to record a program on the DVR, she is not yet in the fluency phase of learning, and that skill is not yet functional. Fluency is what makes a skill useful for a learner.

The **maintenance** phase of learning requires the learner to be able to execute a skill fluently over time without being retaught. Maintenance of a skill can be challenging; this is why teachers sometimes see a decrease in student's expectation-following behavior after weekends and breaks—the students, although fluent with the desired skills, are not yet in the maintenance phase. Remember what you learned in high school? Maybe trigonometry, or French, or scientific notation? Chances are you were in the maintenance phase with some of those skills (maybe long enough to ace a final or be successful on the SAT), but unless you use those skills regularly now, you've since "moved out" of the maintenance phase and might even require reteaching if there were a situation (GREs?) where you'd need those skills again. All instruction should promote skill maintenance so learners can use those skills without reteaching (Simonsen & Myers, 2015).

Finally, the **generalization** phase of learning is the goal of all instruction. In the generalization phase, learners can use a learned skill across settings and time. In addition, learners who reach the generalization phase of learning can modify skills to apply them in new or unusual contexts and situations. For example, an adult may be able to record a program on her DVR, but a real test of generalization comes when a friend asks that adult to record a program on his DVR, which is a different model. Similarly, a student may be able to speak Spanish, but true generalization occurs when that student can converse fluently with native Spanish speakers from Spain, Mexico, Puerto Rico, and Venezuela, all of whom are likely to have different dialects, pronunciations, and idioms.

The goal of all instruction is to ensure that learners become fluent with acquired skills that they can maintain across time and generalize to new settings and situations. We want the readers of this book to meet this goal, and we've already laid some of the groundwork for the acquisition phase by reviewing the basic tenets of CWPBIS earlier in this chapter. All chapters will conclude with questions and activities to promote development at each phase of learning as related to classroom content, and we hope that by the end of the book, you will be able to generalize what you've learned in your own educational environment.

SUGGESTED RESOURCES

In this chapter we have provided a very brief overview of empirically supported classroom management practices, and we want to be sure that you can easily find other resources if you are still in the acquisition or fluency phases of learning about classroom management. We've mentioned two of the resources below earlier in the chapter, so they may sound familiar.

First, the 2015 book *Classwide Positive Behavior Interventions and Supports: A Guide to Proactive Classroom Management*, by Brandi Simonsen and Diane Myers, was the predecessor to the current book and will provide you with an in-depth look at all aspects of CWPBIS. Also, like the current book, each chapter ends with questions and activities to promote successful learning at each phase: acquisition, fluency, maintenance, and generalization.

Second, the 2015 OSEP program brief titled *Supporting and Responding to Behavior: Evidence-Based Classroom Strategies for Teachers* (which can be found at *www.osepideasthatwork.org/evidencebasedclassroomstrategies*) provides an interactive electronic document with clear descriptions, examples, and resources (including videos) that will assist any teacher (in any phase of learning) with the implementation of empirically supported classroom management practices.

Third, the 2016 book *Applied Behavior Analysis for Teachers* (9th edition), by Paul Alberto and Anne Troutman, is one of our favorite resources to recommend for teachers at any phase of learning. All of us have used earlier editions of this textbook to support our own early attempts at effective behavior support in the classroom.

Fourth, The Guilford Practical Intervention in the Schools Series (see title listing at *www.guilford.com/browse/education/guilford-practical-intervention-schools-series*) is designed to support teachers in the classroom and covers a wide variety of relevant instructional, behavioral, and social–emotional topics. Two of our favorite behavior-related titles are *Evidence-Based Practices in Classroom Management* (2017), by David Hulac and Amy Briesch, and *Integrated Multi-Tiered Systems of Support: Blending RTI and PBIS* (2016), by Kent McIntosh and Steve Goodman.

OVERVIEW OF THE BOOK

This book is intended as a guide and resource for those who support teachers (including future and current administrators, current and future school psychologists and related service professionals, providers of professional development, and PBIS teams and coaches). This book will provide necessary information about (1) empirically supported classroom management and behavior support practices, as we've begun to do in this chapter; (2) professional development models that will move teachers toward more systematic implementation; and (3) strategies to support data-based decisions to provide teachers with the most effective support. We envision this book being used in a variety of ways, including:

- An applied text for graduate courses in educational leadership, school psychology, or another field that trains education professionals who will be supporting teachers;
- A resource for teachers who want to enhance their own implementation of empirically supported classroom management practices;
- A guide for school-, district-, or state-level PBIS teams to use when planning the scope and sequence of professional development related to CWPBIS; and
- A handbook for consultants and others who provide professional development for teachers and schools interested in improving classroom management systems.

As you may have already noticed, our book begins with a foreword that provides a historical perspective on PBIS and identifies the need for this book based on current issues in the field of classroom management and behavior support. The book itself is divided into three main sections. Part I describes the foundations of CWPBIS and the phases of learning (which you just read about in this chapter), provides a behavioral framework for supporting adult behavior (Chapter 2), and provides a general overview of implementation supports for teachers (Chapter 3). Part II focuses on empirically supported strategies to support teachers' CWPBIS implementation, including an overview of professional development models (Chapter 4) followed by detailed descriptions and examples of specific strategies, including explicit instruction or training (Chapter 5) and coaching and mentoring (Chapter 6). In Part III, we focus on using data to support teachers before, during, and after professional development, including establishing a data collection system and providing performance feedback (Chapter 7) and data-based differentiation of support for teachers (Chapter 8).

Part I. Supporting Teachers' Implementation of Classwide PBIS: Foundations and Basic Principles

Chapter 1. Foundations of Classwide PBIS

As you've read, Chapter 1 addresses the research-to-practice gap in classroom management and the impact of this gap on students and teachers. We provide an overview of empirically supported classroom management practices, touching briefly on the theoretical foundations of PBIS. We describe the phases of learning and their application to teacher training (and this book), provide a list of additional resources, and explain the need for and organization of this book.

Chapter 2. Behavioral Principles That Impact Adult Behavior Changes

In Chapter 2, we provide a foundation for understanding and deep discussion of behavioral principles relevant to adult behavior change, including the three- and four-term contingencies (i.e., antecedents, behavior, consequences, and setting events and motivating operations). We also examine the behavioral strategies specifically related to supporting teachers' implementation of CWPBIS, including prompting, stimulus control, modeling, shaping, chaining, and programming for generalization.

Chapter 3. Overview of Implementation Supports for Teachers

Chapter 3 begins with an overview of implementation (i.e., phases and drivers of implementation, lessons from research) and follows with considerations for organizing classroom supports for teachers. We revisit empirically supported classroom management practices and then look closely at the foundations and features of the other core PBIS elements (i.e., outcomes, data, systems).

Part II. Empirically Supported Strategies to Support Teachers' Classwide PBIS Implementation

Chapter 4. A Road Map to Building Systems of Support for Teachers

Chapter 4 provides an overview of professional development models, including the typical approaches used to train teachers. We examine empirically supported professional development systems that can be used to support teachers and illustrate how supports for teachers can be organized.

Chapter 5. Designing Effective Training Activities for Classwide PBIS

In Chapter 5, we describe what explicit training looks like and why it is an effective antecedent strategy for supporting teachers. We discuss options for delivery, necessary resources, effective evaluation of explicit instruction, and fidelity of implementation.

Chapter 6. Coaching to Support Teachers' Classwide PBIS Implementation

In Chapter 6, we describe what coaching and mentoring look like and why they are an effective antecedent strategy for supporting teachers. Following the same format as Chapter 5, we discuss options for delivery, necessary resources, effective evaluation of coaching and mentoring, and fidelity of implementation.

Part III. Data-Based Decision Making to Support Teachers' Classwide PBIS Implementation

Chapter 7. Data Collection Systems and Performance Feedback

In Chapter 7, we explore options for efficient and effective data collection and provide examples of relevant tools and checklists. We also discuss how to determine the purpose of data collection and how to use those data to make decisions. In addition, we discuss data-based performance feedback as a consequence strategy, then move into a discussion of options for delivery (e.g., expert, mentor, peer-to-peer).

Chapter 8. Differentiated Supports for Teachers

In Chapter 8, we take a closer look at data-based decision making related to what differentiated (or "tiered") support can look like when training teachers. We discuss the need for differentiated support and provide examples of decision rules and of data-based differential support. We also recap and summarize what we hope you've learned from the book and offer a few considerations for scaling up your support of teachers' CWPBIS implementation.

SUMMARY

Those responsible for training teachers in CWPBIS have a large responsibility. Effective training requires in-depth knowledge of behavioral foundations and principles, of empirically supported classroom management practices, of how the phases of learning affect training, and of how to evaluate the need for, and impact of, training before, during, and after professional development occurs. We hope this book provides content knowledge, support, and a helpful blueprint for those undertaking any teacher training, and we begin by looking closely at the behavioral principles relevant to adult behavior change in Chapter 2.

PHASES OF LEARNING ACTIVITIES: CHAPTER 1

Acquisition

1. Create a checklist of the empirically supported CWPBIS practices described in this chapter that teachers could use to self-evaluate their own CWPBIS implementation. The checklist should include brief descriptions of each included practice and possible examples of what the teacher should be looking for in his or her classroom.

2. Identify each of the four phases of learning and provide a definition and example (related to what teachers' implementation of CWPBIS might look like) for each phase.

Fluency

1. Describe the four core elements of PBIS (i.e., outcomes, systems, data, and practices) to a colleague and check for his or her understanding to evaluate the quality of your description. Specifically, describe how these elements apply to CWPBIS.

2. Design a presentation (e.g., PowerPoint) that summarizes the content of this chapter in a way that would make it clear to your audience and set the stage for learning about supporting teachers' CWPBIS implementation.

Maintenance

1. Review the description of upcoming content provided in this chapter and look at this book's table of contents. Draft a timeline for how you will move through the book. The timeline should be aligned with the phases of learning and your purpose for reading the book. For example, are you reading the book purely for informational purposes, or are you using it to help your school team establish an action plan for CWPBIS implementation in all classrooms? Identify which chapters and content align with the different tasks and steps in your timeline.

2. Review at least two of the other resources we've mentioned in this chapter (e.g., websites such as *www.pbis.org* or some of the other volumes in The Guilford Practical Intervention in the Schools Series). Then make a table that identifies any overlapping content between the resources, as well as any noted differences or unique content. Identify two to three strategies

to ensure that supporting teachers' CWPBIS implementation with different resources is as efficient and effective as possible. That is, how can you avoid redundancy when supporting teachers while (a) maximizing the potential of available resources and (b) giving teachers exposure to different presentations of similar content (which will help program for maintenance and generalization)?

Generalization

1. Select two of the empirically supported CWPBIS practices described in this chapter (e.g., specific praise, error correction, differential reinforcement) and describe how these practices may look when applied to adult behavior. That is, how can CWPBIS practices support teachers' implementation of CWPBIS? (We realize that may be a little confusing, but CWPBIS is ultimately about improving learner outcomes, so how can these practices improve outcomes for our adult learners?)

2. Review the empirically supported CWPBIS practices described in this chapter, then describe any relevant considerations you think would apply when working with teachers to implement those practices in the following settings: (a) a classroom for students who are medically fragile or who have severe disabilities, (b) an alternative school or a juvenile justice facility, and (c) a group home for adults with physical, intellectual, or emotional disabilities.

CHAPTER 2

Behavioral Principles That Impact Adult Behavior Changes

CHAPTER OBJECTIVES

By the end of this chapter, you should be able to . . .

1. Define key behavioral principles (ABCs of behavior) and identify examples of these principles for adults.
2. Describe how behavioral principles can be used to support adult behavior change (i.e., enhance implementation of CWPBIS practices).
3. Begin to apply behavioral principles to prompt, occasion, teach, and reinforce implementation of CWPBIS practices.

Imagine This: You just attended a conference, and you received a ton of recommendations and resources related to effective classroom management. You also heard various stories about how other schools and districts have approached training their teachers in classroom management practices. However, you notice that some of these recommendations and stories seem to contradict each other. As a member of your school leadership team, you would like to be able to make clear recommendations to your team about which classroom management practices to emphasize and how to support teachers in implementing those practices. You've also noticed that teachers within your school and district seem to react differently to training, coaching, and feedback (regardless of the professional development topic). You're not quite sure how to move forward in supporting educators within your school. If only there were a science to guide your decisions about how to support your teachers . . .

THE ABCs OF ADULT BEHAVIOR

Behavioral theory is the science that guides us to make efficient and effective decisions about how to support teachers' implementation of CWPBIS. Behavioral theory explains why people engage in the behaviors they do, and it allows us to predict how they will behave in the future. Even better, behavioral theory helps us change an individual's behavior by changing the environment and providing specific supports. Therefore, if we want to change adult behavior—for instance, if we want to increase teachers' use of CWPBIS practices—we need to understand how to apply behavioral theory.

In Chapter 1, we described how behavioral theory and applied behavioral analysis formed the basis for PBIS. Now, we are ready to apply that theory and describe the basic building blocks of behavior. In this section, we introduce the ABCs (or *antecedents, behaviors*, and *consequences*) of behavior and provide examples of how these building blocks work for a specific subset of adults: educators. Although it typically makes sense to say your ABCs in order, we're going to save antecedents for last, and learn our "BCAs."

Behaviors

Alberto and Troutman (2016) define a behavior as "any observable and measurable act of an individual" (p. 403). When we're referring to a specific act at a specific point in time, we describe that as a "response." However, "behavior" is a better descriptor of actions in general. For example, in a classroom, an educator may ask students, "What sound is this?" after showing *sh* on the smartboard. This one instance (i.e., "What sound is this?") is a teacher **response** known as an opportunity to respond (OTR); however, when you consider the various OTRs that occur throughout that lesson or day, we would describe an OTR as a teacher **behavior** that occasions a student response. (Yes, a teacher behavior can serve as the antecedent for a student behavior. When discussing behavior in a classroom, we need to be clear about whose behavior we mean!) Julie Vargas (B. F. Skinner's daughter and an impressive scholar and scientist in her own right) reminds us that there are two main categories of behavior: **respondent behavior**, which is "controlled by a prior stimulus," and **operant behavior**, which "operates on the environment and is controlled by its immediate effects" (2013, p. 8). Respondent behavior includes involuntary behaviors, often described as instincts or reflexes (e.g., blinking when air blows in your eye). Skinner (1953) describes how, as we evolve, behaviors that increase survival become part of our behavioral repertoire during "evolutionary selection" (p. 90). In contrast, the vast majority of behaviors are voluntary, operant behaviors that are "selected" by their consequences (Skinner, 1953). In other words, operant behaviors "work" (i.e., produce desired or important outcomes) for the individuals engaging in those behaviors.

Walk with us down memory lane. When you were a baby, you likely engaged in many seemingly random behaviors (e.g., body movements, vocalizations), and those behaviors that "worked" for you stayed in your repertoire. For example, think about how a baby may move in different ways. After a few months, she may find that one way of moving (e.g., kicking one leg and arm across her body) may help her move toward a preferred toy. That movement is likely to be repeated, and before long she is rolling to get toward a variety of stimuli, until she learns other movements that allow her to scoot, crawl, or walk. Or a child may be vocalizing various sounds that provide an enjoyable sensation to the child, but the vocalizations "ma-ma" or "da-da" result in high rates of attention from a very important person in that child's life. Those sounds are more likely to be repeated, as they result in increased levels of adult attention.

All organisms have behaviors, and we'll use a few examples from some furry friends in the next sections. However, in this book, we are primarily interested in how teachers behave. The practices described in Chapter 1 are the key teacher behaviors (e.g., teaching routines and expectations, delivering engaging instruction, providing specific feedback) that we want to be sure "work" for the teachers so that these behaviors remain in teachers' repertoires. To ensure that these behaviors work, we have to consider the consequences that follow these behaviors.

Consequences

Consequences are changes in stimuli that occur contingent on a behavior. In behavioral theory, we use the word *stimuli* as a general descriptor that includes activities, attention, sensory stimulation, tangible items, and other features of the environment. To be efficient, we use behavioral notation and abbreviate *stimuli* as a capital S. (As you'll see in the next sections, we use superscripts to denote specific types of stimuli.) Because the word *consequence* is used in various ways in day-to-day life (e.g., "I gave him a consequence"), you may need to erase your current understanding of this word so we can teach you to understand how consequences work in behavioral theory.

Types of Consequences

Consequences can be thought of in two ways. First, we think about the **effect** consequences have on behavior. As we discussed briefly in Chapter 1, consequences may increase the future likelihood of behavior, in which case we say that they strengthen or **reinforce** the behavior. Conversely, consequences may decrease the future likelihood of behavior, in which case we say that they weaken or **punish** the behavior. (If a consequence doesn't have any effect on behavior, it must not be a very interesting or important stimulus change for the person behaving, so we wouldn't still be talking about it!) In behavioral notation, we use a superscript R to indicate a reinforcing stimulus (i.e., S^R) and a superscript P to indicate a punishing stimulus (i.e., S^P).

Second, we can think about *how* the stimulus change occurs, or the **action**. This discussion will likely evoke memories of a middle school math class. When we add, we use a plus (+) sign, and that sign indicates that something is "positive." When we subtract, we use a minus (–) sign, and that sign indicates that something is "negative." We apply this same "signage" to consequences. If the action is to add stimuli to the environment, contingent on behavior, we refer to that as a **positive** consequence. If the action is to remove stimuli from the environment, contingent on behavior, we refer to that as a **negative** consequence. In behavioral notation, the plus and minus also become superscripts to denote the type of reinforcement or punishment. This leads to four types of consequences: positive reinforcement (S^{R+}), negative reinforcement (S^{R-}), positive punishment (S^{P+}), and negative punishment (S^{P-}; see Figure 2.1).

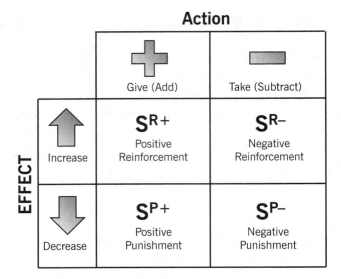

FIGURE 2.1. Four types of consequences based on the action (add/subtract stimuli) and effect (increase/decrease future probability of behavior).

POSITIVE REINFORCEMENT (S^{R+})

Positive reinforcement occurs when a stimulus is added (i.e., given), contingent on behavior, which increases the future probability of a behavior. For example, imagine that Erika raises her hand and a teacher says, "Nice hand-raise, Erika." The teacher added a stimulus (i.e., gave specific praise), and, if Erika is more likely to raise her hand in the future, the teacher positively reinforced Erika's hand-raising behavior. As another example, picture Mr. Green using explicit instruction to teach a concept to a group of students and students providing correct responses to Mr. Green's questions. Students have "given" correct responses, and if Mr. Green continues to teach concepts explicitly, then the students have positively reinforced Mr. Green's instructional behaviors.

NEGATIVE REINFORCEMENT (S^{R-})

Negative reinforcement occurs when a stimulus is subtracted (i.e., taken away), contingent on behavior, which increases the future probability of a behavior. For example, Theo is a student who is talking loudly with a peer instead of listening to a teacher's instruction—a behavior that most teachers find pretty aversive. While moving around the classroom actively supervising students, Ms. Reiner taps on Theo's desk and tugs her ear (a signal that she pretaught to redirect him to listen to her instruction). Theo immediately stops talking and orients his body, eyes, and ears toward the teacher. Thus, contingent on Ms. Reiner's behavior (i.e., the redirection), Theo has removed an aversive stimulus (i.e., talking loudly) from the environment. If Ms. Reiner is more likely to use redirections in the future, then we would describe this as an example of negative reinforcement.

POSITIVE PUNISHMENT (S^{P+})

Positive punishment occurs when a stimulus is added (i.e., given), contingent on behavior, which decreases the future probability of a behavior. For example, imagine Kiya, a preschool student, trying to forcefully pull a toy out of her peer's hand (student behavior). Kiya's teacher provides a quick error correction (i.e., adds a stimulus): "Kiya, that is not safe. Use words to ask your friend to share." If, after being given an error correction, Kiya is less likely to use physical force to get objects in the future (i.e., the behavior decreases), then Kiya's behavior was positively punished. As another example, when the same teacher gives an error correction (teacher behavior) to Kiya's peer Brian, he escalates into a full tantrum (i.e., screaming, kicking, and throwing himself on the floor—adding multiple stimuli at the same time). If the teacher is less likely to correct Brian in the future (i.e., the behavior decreases), Brian has positively punished the teacher's "error correction" behavior. (Now, ask yourself what effect Kiya's response had on the teacher's error correction behavior. If you realized that Kiya's decreasing her behavior—i.e., removing stimuli—may have negatively reinforced the teachers' behavior, you'd be correct, but only if the teacher continued to use error corrections with Kiya.)

Let's look at one more example. Imagine a history teacher looking out at his well-behaved high school students who are eagerly awaiting his instruction. He tells them that they are going to try something new and move into cooperative learning groups to debate the true causes of the U.S. Civil War (teacher behavior). Within 5 minutes, his classroom erupts into chaos, with students arguing loudly about whether the cause was slavery or states' rights (students adding aversive stimuli), and he decides he'll never use cooperative groups again (teacher behavior decreases; his behavior was positively punished by the students' arguing). As a side note, perhaps you noticed a way this teacher could have increased the likelihood of students' success. Teachers should only introduce new instructional routines *after* teaching or reteaching expectations! Cooperative learning groups can be an effective strategy *if* students have been explicitly taught how to engage in them.

NEGATIVE PUNISHMENT (S^{P-})

Negative punishment occurs when a stimulus is subtracted (i.e., taken away), contingent on behavior, which decreases the future probability of a behavior. For example, in the previous scenario, Kiya's teacher may have removed the toy (rather than delivering an error correction). If removing the toy decreased Kiya's future "toy pulling" behavior, then the teacher effectively used negative punishment. As you may have already guessed, negative punishment also works for teachers. Consider this scenario: Ms. Lopez and Chonté have a history of positive interactions about Chonté's strong writing in her ninth-grade English class. Ms. Lopez often provides written or private feedback to Chonté about her strengths. On Monday, Chonté has a pleasant affect and orients her body toward the front of the room as Ms. Lopez introduces a new writing assignment. Ms. Lopez then says she is going to read an exemplar paper and proceeds to read an excerpt of Chonté's last assignment, publicly acknowledging Chonté's strengths (teacher behavior). Chonté's affect immediately changes—she looks down, withdraws eye contact, and avoids the teacher at the end of class when they would typically have a private chat (i.e., Chonté withdraws her attention). If Ms. Lopez is less likely to publicly acknowledge Chonté in the future, Ms. Lopez's behavior has been negatively punished.

Function of Behavior

Now, hopefully, with the clear definitions and examples, you are fluent with the four types of consequences. However, many people (and, unfortunately, popular media) often confuse these concepts—especially negative reinforcement and positive punishment. Therefore, we need a simpler way to talk about consequences in our everyday life, especially when we are trying to understand why behaviors keep happening. When an individual continues to engage in behaviors across time, we have learned that those behaviors "work" for that individual or, in behavioral terms, that those behaviors have been reinforced. As we just learned, reinforcement can happen when stimuli are added (i.e., positive reinforcement) or subtracted (i.e., negative reinforcement) contingent on behavior.

To simplify our language, we talk about behaviors serving a **function**, or purpose, for an individual. There are two specific functions: (1) to **get or obtain** access to desired attention, objects, activities, sensory stimulation, or other stimuli and (2) to **escape or avoid** undesired attention, objects, activities, sensory stimulation, or other stimuli. Now, if you're thinking that sounds a lot like positive and negative reinforcement, you're right. Function of behavior is nothing more than describing a history or pattern of positive (i.e., to get or obtain) or negative (i.e., to escape or avoid) reinforcement across time.

We typically apply the concept of function to students' problematic behaviors. For example, we may conduct a functional behavioral assessment to document the pattern of reinforcement (positive or negative) for a students' behavior and develop a function-based behavior support plan. However, all behaviors serve a function. That is, desired and undesired behaviors, students' and teachers' behaviors, and even administrators' behaviors serve a function. Therefore, we could think about a teacher (e.g., Mr. Green from our earlier example) engaging in explicit instruction to increase the probability of (i.e., get or obtain) students' correct academic responding. We could also think about another teacher (e.g., Ms. Reiner from our earlier example) engaging in effective redirection strategies to escape challenging student behavior.

Although we've been using examples of desired teacher behaviors (primarily classroom management practices), undesired teacher behaviors serve a function as well. For example, a teacher may yell and shame students (instead of correcting or redirecting) to escape aversive challenging behavior, and this response is especially likely if the teacher hasn't been taught more positive and proactive ways to prevent and respond to challenging behavior. When supporting teachers, we need to be aware of, first, their prior training (i.e., What practices do they know?); second, their prior learning history (i.e., Which practices have worked for them in the past?); and, third, the current contingencies in their classrooms that may be reinforcing (or punishing) different CWPBIS practices (i.e., What's working for them now?). In short, we always need to "think functionally" about behavior, whether we're hoping to increase effective practices, decrease ineffective practices, or support other teacher behaviors related to improving student outcomes.

Extinction of Behavior

There's one other consequence situation that we need to consider: What happens when a behavior that has been working for someone stops working? That is, what happens when a behavior that has been previously reinforced is no longer reinforced? The short answer is **extinction**: The behavior eventually disappears. In some cases, extinction is a good thing. Imagine a student who has been engaging in a disruptive behavior to get her teacher's attention, and the teacher (1) teaches the student a more effective way to get attention (e.g., asking for help) and (2) ignores the disruptive behavior (e.g., withholds attention from a behavior previously reinforced by attention). If the teacher is consistent in withholding his or her attention (i.e., extinction), the disruptive behavior will eventually disappear. Extinction can be used in conjunction with differential reinforcement of alternative behaviors (DRA; see Chapter 1) and noncontingent reinforcement.

Occasionally, behavior gets worse before it disappears, and this temporary increase is known as an **extinction burst**. Although the burst is temporary, "temporary" may feel like forever with particularly disruptive behaviors. When deciding to put a behavior on extinction, the teacher should determine whether she or he can withstand the extinction burst (e.g., What if the behavior targeted for extinction is loud cursing that functions to obtain peer attention? Imagine what even a temporary increase in that behavior could do to the classroom environment!) and whether any potential disruptions are too great. If so, she or he may want to select another strategy to decrease inappropriate behavior. Remember, extinction bursts are natural, functional, and somewhat predictable; it's up to the teacher to determine what is most appropriate in a particular situation.

Extinction, like all other behavioral concepts, also works for teachers. Imagine that a teacher begins the year with an effectively implemented token economy recognition system in which students earn tickets and can exchange them for items on a class menu. In September and October, her students respond to the system (i.e., their desired behaviors consistently increase; the system is reinforcing desired behaviors). But around the middle of November, the system seems to stop working. Students say they don't care, they are leaving tickets on the floor, and their problem behavior is increasing. The teacher may temporarily increase her ticket distribution (i.e., extinction burst), but she ultimately gives up and stops using the system. The behaviors involved with implementing her recognition system, like dinosaurs, are now extinct! Unlike dinosaurs, though, we can "revive" behaviors that have undergone extinction by reinforcing them (either purposefully, if those behaviors are desired, or accidentally, if the behaviors are undesired). As you probably suspected, we have several recommendations this teacher could try before giving up her recognition system. For starters, she could reteach skills, ask students what they would like to earn, modify the available reinforcers, and change how tickets are distributed to try to reestablish the reinforcing properties for students and the teacher.

Unfortunately, like our example teacher, some teachers give up their system and say recognition doesn't work simply because their recognition behaviors have undergone an extinction process. A better understanding of behavioral theory—and some of the data collection strategies discussed in Chapter 7—could help prevent this hasty abandonment of a system that likely took substantial effort to implement and had a pretty solid record of success.

Antecedents

Now that we've learned B and C, it's time to go back to A. Antecedents are any stimuli that precede a behavior. As most college undergraduates learn from Pavlov (usually in their introductory psychology course), antecedents can elicit behaviors if they are unconditioned (e.g., the presence of food elicits drooling) or as a result of respondent conditioning. However, B. F. Skinner taught us (many of us for the first time in that same introductory psych course) that many antecedents primarily affect behavior due to their history of association with specific consequences.

Types of Antecedents

In Skinner's description of operant conditioning, there are three main types of antecedents: *discriminative stimuli*, *stimuli delta*, and *discriminative stimuli minus*. As we did in our discussion of consequences, we continue to use a capital S to represent a stimulus, and we now use superscripts (i.e., ^{D}, $^\Delta$, and $^{D-}$, respectively) to indicate the type of antecedent stimuli.

DISCRIMINATIVE STIMULI (S^D)

Antecedent stimuli that were present when a behavior was reinforced in the past are likely to "signal" the availability of reinforcement and occasion similar behaviors in the future (note that we say "occasion," not "elicit," as the behavior is voluntary). In behavioral notation, we use the superscript D to denote discriminative stimuli (i.e., S^D). When scientists originally studied behavioral principles in animal labs, they placed hungry rats in an operant conditioning chamber, also known as a "Skinner box." The box was set up with a lever at one end, a food tray in close proximity, and a light; when rats pressed the lever, a food pellet was delivered into the tray. Quickly, rats learned to press the lever to receive a food pellet; presentation of the food pellet increased (i.e., reinforced) future "lever pressing" behavior. When scientists made food available only when the light was on, the rats began to press the lever only when the light was on. The light functioned as a discriminative stimulus (i.e., S^D) signaling the availability of food, and the process of the rat learning to press the bar only in the presence of the light is called discrimination training (see Figure 2.2). We discuss discrimination training later in this chapter.

Now that you're imagining rats in boxes, we'd like to bring you back to the human world and point out that discriminative stimuli exist throughout our environment and affect our behavior. For example, many of you likely have set distinctive ringtones on your cellphones

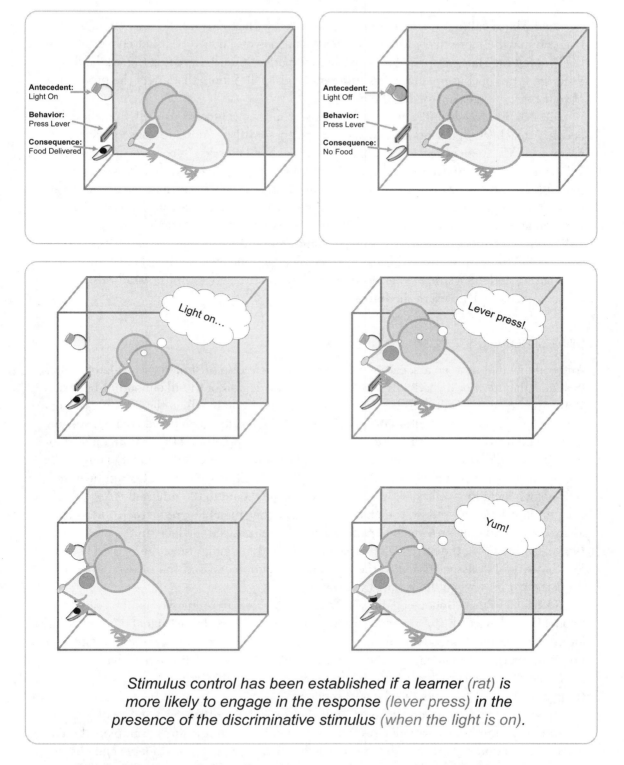

*Stimulus control has been established if a learner (rat) is
more likely to engage in the response (lever press) in the
presence of the discriminative stimulus (when the light is on).*

FIGURE 2.2. Illustration of using discrimination training (light on/off) to establish stimulus control for a rat's "lever-pressing" behavior.

to signal who is calling. If the ringtone is associated with a person to whom you enjoy talking, you may be more likely to pick up the phone, as you know a pleasant conversation is likely to follow. Thus, your ringtones are discriminative stimuli, signaling the availability of different types of consequences (i.e., different types of attention) that affect the probability of your behavior (i.e., answering the phone).

Discriminative stimuli are present in classroom environments as well, and they may occasion teachers' behaviors due to their association with reinforcing consequences. For example, if Ms. Reen greets Joaquin (i.e., S^D) at the door and says, "Good morning" (teacher behavior), and Joaquin smiles and says, "Thanks! Good morning to you," Ms. Reen may be more likely to greet Joaquin (or similar students) in the future if she enjoys Joaquin's pleasant reciprocal greeting (i.e., the possibility of receiving a similar pleasant reciprocal greeting increases the likelihood that she will greet other students at the door in the future). In a different classroom, a student raises her hand (S^D) and Mr. Xu provides specific praise (teacher behavior). If he experiences that students continue to raise their hands (instead of talking out) and enjoys this experience, he may be more likely to praise hand raising (and other expected behaviors) in the future.

STIMULI DELTA (S^Δ)

Antecedents that have no association with reinforcement or punishment are called S-deltas (S^Δ), and they do not directly affect (i.e., increase or decrease) the likelihood of behavior. Returning to our rat friend in the Skinner box, the condition in which the S^D is not present (i.e., no light) is the S^Δ condition (Cooper et al., 2007). In an instructional context, specific S^Δs may be introduced as "distractor" stimuli to increase precision of discrimination training. For example, if scientists wanted rats to pay attention to the color of light and only press the bar when the yellow light was illuminated, they might use a light that could turn multiple colors, including yellow. Then they would expose the rat to the different colors of light (e.g., initially blue and yellow; then blue, red, and yellow; then blue, red, green, and yellow; and so forth) and only provide food pellets when the rat pressed the lever in the presence of the yellow light (i.e., the S^D). The other colors of light (blue, red, green, etc.) would become S^Δs that were not associated with the presence of reinforcers, and the rat would learn to press the bar only when the yellow light was on.

Consider your cellphone again. Every now and then, an unknown number calls your phone. If you have no history with a number, the number likely doesn't signal that a pleasant (or aversive) interaction would follow. Therefore, your behavior of answering the phone (or not) is unlikely to be related to that particular number. (Of course, if you have had a history of aversive experiences when answering unknown numbers, this stimulus may signal something else, as we'll talk about in the next section.)

In a classroom, there are many stimuli that do not signal the availability of pleasant (or aversive) stimuli for particular responses. As a silly (but illustrative) example, a botany teacher may regularly use specific praise (teacher behavior) with her students and observe increases in the praised behaviors over time (i.e., desired student behavior increases, positively reinforcing the teachers' use of specific praise). Given how fluent this behavior (i.e., specific praise) is for the teacher, she may find herself talking with (and then praising) her classroom plants. Obviously, the plants do not give her immediate feedback that reinforces her praising behavior, and the plants' lack of response is unlikely to maintain or increase her "plant-praising" behavior. As a less silly (but also illustrative) example, there may be students who do not immediately respond to (i.e., reinforce) the teacher's specific praise, and we may worry that, as with her plants, the teacher may be less likely to praise these students in the future. As we discussed in Chapter 1, praise is a non-negotiable strategy for your classroom. Therefore, it's critical to implement your own strategies to make sure that you are distributing specific praise to all students, contingent on their desired behaviors, even if some of them don't immediately reinforce (i.e., respond by increasing desired behaviors) your praising behavior.

DISCRIMINATIVE STIMULI MINUS (S^{D-})

Antecedent stimuli that were present when a behavior was punished in the past are likely to "signal" the possibility of punishment and decrease the likelihood of similar behavior in their presence. Now, we would never harm rats (nor would Skinner), but some people do use punishment to train their dogs to stay in their yards (e.g., an electric fence). People set up an electric boundary that consistently delivers an aversive electric shock each time a dog crosses the boundary while wearing a shock collar. The stimuli associated with the edge of that boundary (e.g., edge of lawn, sidewalk) become discriminative stimuli for punishment (or S^{D-}) when a dog consistently experiences an aversive stimulus (e.g., electric shock) in the presence of those stimuli. The dog avoids approaching the stimuli, and "boundary-crossing behavior" decreases.

In our day-to-day interactions with humans, we don't use electric shock collars, but we do experience a variety of punishers (e.g., aversive attention, activities, stimulation) in the presence of certain stimuli, and we learn to avoid the stimuli (and thus punishers associated with these situations). Let's return to the cellphone example. If you have a contentious relationship with a colleague, his or her ringtone (or number on your phone's screen) may signal the availability of aversive attention if you answer the phone. Therefore, you may be less likely to answer the phone if you hear or see stimuli signaling that particular colleague is calling.

In a classroom setting, there are also S^{D-}s that may decrease an educator's behavior in certain circumstances. For example, Ms. Newman has a great relationship with most families in her classroom, but Mr. Oscar (a father of one of her students) starts and ends most communications with grouchy and loud (e.g., all CAPS in an email) communication about something the teacher has done wrong. Although Ms. Newman may look forward to emailing most families, she may be less likely to reach out to Mr. Oscar, as she knows that an aversive communication is likely to result. As another example, Mr. Akbar finds that many of his students enjoy his academic instruction, including his fast-paced strategies to invite their participation. (He provides opportunities to respond at a rate of three to five OTRs per minute!) However, when Mr. Akbar gives Joe an opportunity to participate, Joe clenches his jaw, pushes his materials away, and puts his head down. If Mr. Akbar continues to present OTRs to Joe, Joe may tip over his desk and leave the room (as he has done before). Over time, Mr. Akbar finds that he is much less likely to attempt to engage Joe in his instruction. In these examples, Mr. Oscar and Joe have become S^{D-}s, signaling the availability of punishers and decreasing the likelihood of previously punished behaviors (i.e., contacting families and student-specific OTRs, respectively).

Stimulus Control

Taken together, the three types of antecedents (S^D, S^Δ, and S^{D-}) signal the availability of different consequence conditions for a particular response. Therefore, a learner becomes more likely to engage in that response in the presence of the S^D than in its absence (i.e., S^Δ), and even less likely to engage in the response if an S^{D-} is present. In the next section, we talk about how to purposefully establish stimulus control. However, as many of the previous examples illustrated, our behaviors also come under stimulus control (even though it hasn't been purposefully established by anyone). Consider one teacher behavior (e.g., providing specific praise when students raise their hands) as an example. Can you identify how the types of antecedent stimuli (S^D, S^Δ, and S^{D-}) may operate in a classroom in which students presently talk out about as often as they raise their hands? First, a student raising her hand should be an S^D that occasions teacher praise (e.g., "Thank you for raising your hand"), and this praising likely increases hand-raises and decreases talk-outs in the future (reinforcing the behavior of giving specific praise). Second, a teacher may mistakenly praise a student who is stretching (not raising a hand). That praise likely has no effect on hand-raising (or stretching) behavior, as it wasn't delivered contingent on an actual hand-raise. Therefore, stretching is an S^Δ. Finally, if a teacher said "Thank you for raising your hand" when a student talked out, likely (1) the teacher was sarcastic instead of genuine (not a good idea!) and (2) the student reacted by talking out more. Therefore, a talk-out functions as an S^{D-} for teacher praise (see Figure 2.3). A better response to a talk-out would be to redirect the student to raise her hand, so a talk-out may function as an S^D for redirecting behavior, resulting in a decrease in talk-outs.

Setting Events and Motivating Operations

Have you ever noticed that some days are harder than others, even when most of the stimuli in your environment (e.g., physical structures, routines, consequences) are similar? Perhaps, on a particularly difficult day, you didn't get enough sleep and you're tired, or you skipped breakfast and you're hungry, or you had a fight with someone. Or perhaps you got a huge raise and you're so excited you're having a hard time focusing. These temporary antecedent conditions (e.g., tired, hungry) or events (e.g., fight, raise) affect your behavior in a different way from the antecedent stimuli we've already discussed: They don't signal the availability of different consequences in your immediate environment, but they may change the value

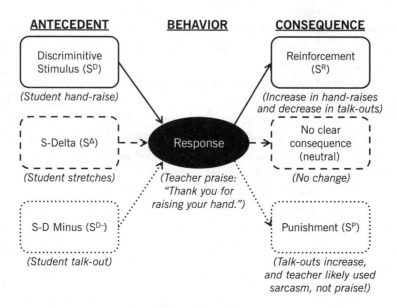

FIGURE 2.3. Types of antecedent stimuli and their relationship with specific consequences (with an example related to a teacher's specific praise behavior).

or effectiveness of those consequences. For example, if you're tired, the reinforcers for arriving to work on time (e.g., getting copies done before there's a line) may be less effective than those for stopping by your favorite coffee or tea shop (i.e., caffeine). So you may alter your behavior (e.g., stopping for coffee instead of driving straight to work) based on the consequences that are the most effective at the moment, even though the other stimuli haven't changed (i.e., the clock still tells you it's time to go to work, and the coffee shop is always on your way to work).

In behavioral terms, we describe these temporary conditions or events as "setting events" (Bijou & Baer, 1961) or "motivating operations" (Laraway, Snycerski, Michael, & Poling, 2003). Each of these terms originated from different groups of scientists who describe them slightly differently (Horner, Vaughn, Day, & Ard, 1996); however, those differences are so slight that we'll consider them to be similar and use the term *setting events*. The key defining features of setting events are that they (1) are **temporary** conditions or events that (2) affect behavior by **altering the value or effectiveness** of consequences. As the examples illustrate, setting events may be present at the same time as the immediate S^D (e.g., tired, hungry), or setting events may happen before (sometimes hours or days before) the immediate S^D (e.g., fight, raise). A variety of stimuli may function as setting events; for example, setting events may be physical (e.g., fatigue, hunger, sickness, pain), social (e.g., negative or positive interactions), environmental (e.g., changes in sound, light, temperature, or other physical stimuli), or some combination thereof (e.g., increased smoke from wildfires may cause physical and other symptoms for some individuals). However, conditions that are not temporary (e.g., disability, mental health condition) are *not* setting events, although their symptoms may be. For example, someone may have schizophrenia (not a setting event) and occasionally have visual and auditory hallucinations (temporary events that may be setting events) that affect behavior.

Setting events present unique challenges for educators; sometimes, teachers don't even know that they've occurred. When teachers are aware of setting events, how they respond depends on the student, the situation, and the event itself. Sometimes, setting events can be eliminated (e.g., if a student has frequent fights on the bus, alternative transportation to school can be arranged). Other times, teachers may need to mitigate the effects of a setting event (e.g., allowing a student to work alone quietly after a weekend babysitting multiple siblings) or eliminate an antecedent that has the potential to occasion inappropriate behavior (e.g., if group work often occasions tantrums even when setting events aren't present, the teacher may allow a student to work alone if a setting event has occurred). Sometimes, the teacher can provide additional reinforcement to counteract the impact of the setting event; for example, if a student has a fight with a parent on state testing day (and tests have the potential to occasion inappropriate behavior), the teacher may say, "Alexis, I know you've had a difficult morning. It's state testing day and if you can meet all expectations and stay on task during the test, you can have time to play your favorite computer game this afternoon." While these are not intended to be long-term solutions, awareness of and appropriate responses to setting events can decrease the likelihood of challenging behavior in the classroom.

Summary of ABCs

In the previous sections, we've described a four-term contingency that explains how antecedents and consequences affect operant behaviors (see Figure 2.4). Specifically, **behaviors** are observable and measurable actions, **consequences** increase (i.e., S^R) or decrease (i.e., S^P) the future probability of behaviors, and **antecedents** signal the differential availability (i.e., S^D, S^Δ, and S^{D-}) and determine the value or effectiveness (setting events) of consequences in that moment.

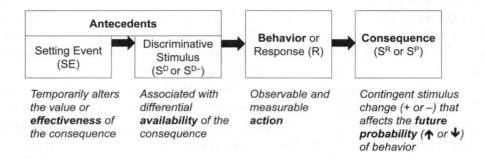

FIGURE 2.4. The four-term contingency that describes how antecedents (setting events and discriminative stimuli) and consequences (reinforcement and punishment) affect behavior.

BEHAVIORAL STRATEGIES INVOLVED IN SUPPORTING TEACHERS' IMPLEMENTATION OF CWPBIS

Now that we've learned our ABCs, we can think about how to apply these principles to supporting teachers' implementation of CWPBIS practices. Remember that CWPBIS practices are the key teacher behaviors we want to make sure "work" for teachers in the classroom, as decades of research have documented that these practices work for students. As we described in Chapter 1 (and discuss again in upcoming chapters), many teachers arrive in the field without sufficient training in classroom practices; therefore, we may need to consider how we will train new teacher behaviors. Other practices, such as providing prompts, may be behaviors teachers have learned, but those behaviors may not be occurring under the correct stimulus conditions; therefore, we may need to purposefully establish stimulus control for these behaviors. We also want teachers to implement practices in different instructional routines (e.g., while teaching math, during transitions) and differentiate those practices to meet the needs of all students. In terms of phases of learning, this means we need to program for **generalization** to help teachers implement their practices across contexts and adapt (i.e., differentiate) their practices to meet the needs of all learners. Finally, we know that supporting teachers' implementation of evidence-based practices can be challenging. Therefore, we need to think about how we can prompt and reinforce teachers' implementation of CWPBIS practices.

Training New Behaviors

From a behavioral perspective, there are two main procedures for training new behaviors. When the behaviors are simple or a group of behaviors are expected to be displayed simultaneously (e.g., eye contact, pleasant affect, and specific verbal praise), we use shaping. When behaviors are complex or expected to be displayed as a sequence (e.g., teaching social skills), we use chaining. Although you've likely heard these terms applied to how we teach students, these same concepts are critical in training and supporting teachers.

Shaping

Many of the CWPBIS practices are relatively simple (e.g., providing specific praise), but the challenge lies in having a teacher skillfully and fluently implement these practices at a rate that improves student outcomes. Although it's critical to teach directly what these skills look like (i.e., by defining them, modeling them, and providing examples and non-examples), the typical procedure we use to coach teachers in using these skills involves shaping.

Shaping is systematically reinforcing successive approximations of the desired behavior (Alberto & Troutman, 2016). Shaping begins with identifying a skill the learner currently exhibits, identifying what the target or desired behavior looks like, and then determining the path to get from current to desired behavior, that is, which key behavior changes or "approximations" should be reinforced. For example, after introducing the idea of specific praise, you notice that a teacher currently provides general praise ("Good!") or gestures (thumbs-up, high-fives) to recognize correct academic responses or desired social behaviors. Each time the teacher provides slightly more descriptive praise (e.g., "Good work") you provide an acknowledgment (e.g., "I saw that you were trying to label the behavior [student correct academic responding] when you said, 'Good work' "). Over time, you shift to providing positive feedback only when the teacher actually used specific praise for correct academic responding (e.g., the teacher says, "That's correct! A triangle with three equal sides is an equilateral triangle") or desired behavior (e.g., the teacher says, "Thanks for entering quietly. That was respectful of your peers who were already working").

After you've shaped what the teacher's practice looked like (or the "topography" of the behavior), you may shift your focus to a different **dimension** of the behavior appropriate for the target practice. For example, you may want to work with a teacher on increasing her rate of specific praise. You may initially reinforce her current rate (e.g., "You're providing specific praise about once every 3 minutes. Great start to making praise more effective in your classroom!"), but over time you shift reinforcement to higher and higher rates, until the teacher hits her desired rate (e.g., "Wow, you're praising students about once a minute. You can see the improvements in the students' behavior!").

You may also look at how a teacher is distributing his or her practice across students in the classroom and shape a more appropriate distribution. For example, teachers should distribute positive and proactive practices equally among students with different demographic characteristics (e.g., race/ethnicity, gender identity) but unequally among students with different needs. Students with more intensive needs should experience higher (not lower!) rates of positive and proactive CWPBIS practices. Research shows students with more intensive needs often receive fewer positive and proactive supports; therefore, this may be a good area to "shape" when supporting teachers' implementation of CWPBIS practices.

Chaining

Other CWPBIS practices are a bit more complex and require teachers to implement a sequence of behaviors to execute the practice effectively. For example, teaching an effective, explicit social skills lesson involves modeling, providing guided practice (i.e., leading), and evaluating the effect of instruction (i.e., testing). Delivering an effective error correction also involves a multistep sequence: (1) signaling the error (e.g., "That looked like running"), (2) identifying the correct response (e.g., "We walk when entering the class to be safe"), (3) providing an opportunity to practice with feedback (e.g., "Please go back and show me how you walk." [Student walks.] "Nice walking!"), and (4) disengaging (e.g., "Now, let's get started with our 'do now' work"). When practices involve multiple steps, we need to first perform a **task analysis** to identify the critical steps involved in the practice (as we just described for teaching and error correction) and then teach the steps in the task using **chaining**.

A task analysis involves breaking a task down into its component parts. To perform a task analysis for CWPBIS practices, you may start with the critical features (as described in Chapter 1) and watch a range of "experts" implement the practices in their setting. That way, you'll be able to identify and describe the common steps required to implement the practice effectively. When performing a task analysis, it's also important to know the learning history of your audience. For example, if you're training a group of educators who don't have a background in explicit instruction, you may need to further break down and describe the steps involved in the model–lead–test process. However, if you're training a group of educators who are experts at explicit academic instruction, you could just train what those "chunks" look like for teaching social skills.

Furthermore, there are some skills you'd want to train step by step, through a chaining process. When teaching error corrections, for example, we may initially ask teachers to practice how they would signal a student's error. Some teachers need help doing this in a way that is calm, neutral, and business-like (i.e., the most effective way to signal an error). After teachers have this first step mastered, we have teachers practice identifying and stating what they'd like the student to do instead. Once teachers are able to do those two steps, we have them practice asking students to practice the new behavior and then practice disengaging from the student. Thus, we build each component of the "error-correction chain" until the teacher is successfully able to deliver the error correction in a training context.

We may also use chaining for skills that have bigger "chunks." When we work with schools to implement social skills training, for example, we often start by having teachers work to define the desired social behaviors in the context of their classroom expectations and routines. Once teachers have clear definitions, we have them plan how they will explicitly teach (i.e., model–lead–test) expected behaviors, or social skills, at the beginning of the school year. Then we ask teachers to develop a whole-year plan to teach, review, and revisit social skills throughout the school year. And, depending on the teachers' learning history, we may further break down these tasks.

Technically, you can chain tasks using (1) *forward* chaining, by starting with the first step (as our examples illustrate); (2) *backward* chaining, by starting with the last step and working backward to build the chain; or (3) *total task presentation*, by having teachers practice the whole sequence each time with varying amounts of support. Although you may need backward chaining or total task presentation for a specific skill or learner, most of the examples from our training employ forward chaining.

Establishing Stimulus Control

As we described, shaping and chaining are ways to teach new behaviors (i.e., practices that are not already in a teacher's repertoire). However, a teacher may already know how to do a practice but is not using it under the correct stimulus conditions. Consider a teacher who knows it's important to prompt desired student behavior but who often waits until the first student makes an error before remembering to, first, correct that student and, second, provide a general reminder to the whole class. The teacher clearly has the skill of providing a reminder, but he isn't doing it under the correct stimulus conditions (i.e., at the beginning of each activity rather than after a student error). Therefore, our training goal is to establish stimulus control by ensuring that the appropriate stimuli (i.e., beginning of new or challenging activity/routine) occasion the response (i.e., the teacher prompting desired student behavior).

In this process, we first need to be sure that teachers are aware of (1) S^Ds (e.g., "It's important to provide prompts at the beginning of each new or challenging routine"), (2) potential reinforcers (e.g., "Evidence suggests that providing a brief reminder or prompt decreases disruptive behavior and increases appropriate behavior"), and (3) the efficiency of the behavior (e.g., "Given that you typically provide reminders after an error correction, precorrecting will be faster and likely save the time you spend correcting the behavior!"). In other words, you train the ABCs. Then teachers actually need to experience these ABCs. Additionally, as teachers are learning this new skill, we may need to add reminders (i.e., prompts for prompts!) and reinforcers to increase the likelihood of teachers' success. For example, if we are providing coaching as described in Chapter 6, we may remind the teacher to begin her lesson with a prompt for expected behavior. Then, after the teacher does it, we may write a sticky note that says, "Great way to remind your students about raising their hands. In the first 5 minutes of instruction, I counted 10 quiet hand-raises for every talk-out. So, clearly your prompt was effective!" We may then leave the note to increase the likelihood that the teacher experiences reinforcement (i.e., positive peer attention, increased desired student behavior, and decreased undesired student behavior).

Furthermore, to ensure that we have established stimulus control, we need to consider not only when the behavior should occur (i.e., S^D) but also when it should not occur (i.e., S^Δ and S^{D-}). We should also think about other potential behaviors that could compete with the desired behavior in the presence of the same S^D. For instance, to return to our example of prompting, it is possible to prompt too much. Although we'd like teachers to provide prompts for expected behaviors at the beginning of new and challenging routines, we don't want to train teachers to prompt throughout the routine or to continue prompting after a routine has become fluent or easy for students. Our goal is actually to fade prompting so that the natural S^D occasions the desired behavior. Therefore, we want to use non-examples in training to teach the critical features of the S^D (i.e., a **new** or **challenging** routine or activity for which teachers should prompt) and contrast those examples with other S^Δs (i.e., in a learned routine or activity for which students already engage in expected behavior, teachers should not prompt). Furthermore, we want to consider other behaviors teachers could engage in at the beginning of a new or challenging routine (e.g., reviewing instructional materials, responding to an email) that may interfere with their ability to prompt effectively; for instance, we can suggest to teachers that they arrange their environment to ensure that these behaviors happen at a different time. Finally, when coaching, we want to reinforce (e.g., provide praise on sticky notes) only when prompting happened in the presence of the S^D (i.e., at the beginning of a new or challenging routine). We would not reinforce when prompting happened in other conditions (i.e., S^Δ)—for example, saying "Remember to line up quietly" when students are already doing so—or if other behaviors occurred in the presence of the S^D—for example, the teacher says "Don't talk" when students begin filing into the classroom (an S^D for prompting), instead of prompting students to sit and quietly begin working. This process is called discrimination training (training teachers to discriminate between S^D and S^Δ and bring the correct responses under control of the S^D). Remember, Figure 2.2 depicts a rat-based example of discrimination training.

Now, you may be asking yourself whether it's appropriate to use punishment when establishing stimulus control. If you're thinking of an aversive consequence (e.g., electric shock), the answer is an obvious and resounding "No!" But it may be appropriate to deliver corrective feedback to decrease the likelihood of a teacher engaging in other behaviors in the presence of the S^D or performing the trained behavior in the incorrect situations. If we're introducing punishment, these incorrect situations would now become S^{D-}s, signaling that punishment is available. Returning to the previous example, we'd still want to reinforce (e.g., provide praise via sticky note) only when prompting happened in the presence of the S^D (at the beginning of a new or challenging routine), and we would now correct (i.e., privately debrief and remind the teacher about when to prompt) when prompting happened in other conditions (S^{D-}s) or if other behaviors occurred in the presence of the S^D. Whether using an S^Δ or S^{D-} condition, the process of establishing stimulus control creates a very "tight" relationship within the ABC part of the four-term contingency. The behavior has been trained to occur in the presence of the S^D to result in S^R. (Congratulations, by the way—you're now reading in behavioral shorthand!) To maximize the effects of your training, you want to ensure that the setting events in effect during your training are similar to those in the natural environment. For example, if you're training after a long school day, you may want to provide coffee, water, and snacks so teachers are not excessively tired, thirsty, or hungry. Or you may insert short trainings into existing meetings that occur throughout the school day, such as grade-level or department meetings. In short, you want to consider the full four-term contingency (i.e., setting event → antecedent → behavior → consequence) when establishing stimulus control.

Programming for Generalization

We just learned about stimulus control, which emphasizes discrimination; that is, responding in a certain way (i.e., response, or R) in the presence of specific stimuli (S^D) to produce reinforcement. If you think about a continuum that starts with discrimination on one end (i.e., 1:1 correspondence between S^D and R), the opposite end of the continuum would be generalization (which, as we've mentioned previously, is the goal of all teaching). When supporting teachers, we want a balance between discrimination and generalization. We don't actually want to train only one individual S^D and R relationship, or we'd have to train a teacher to respond to each and every unique S^D with a unique response. To make our training more efficient, we want to train teachers to respond to common S^Ds with common responses. For example, we want to train teachers to prompt in a variety of ways (i.e., group of responses) at the beginning of all new or challenging routines or activities (i.e., a group of stimuli that share a common discriminative property). To describe these "groups" of responses or stimuli, we will use the word *class*. A **stimulus class** is a group of stimuli that share common properties and would be expected to occasion similar responses. A response class is a group of behaviors that result in similar types of consequences (e.g., positive or negative reinforcement). Therefore, we typically want learners to respond to all members of a stimulus class, and we want them to select or adapt a response from a member of the appropriate response class.

To promote generalization, we need to purposefully program for it using **general case programming** (Horner & Albin, 1988). General case programming starts by identifying the range of stimulus examples that are within the desired stimulus class (e.g., new or challenging routines or activities). It's also important to identify stimulus examples that are not members of that class (e.g., examples of familiar and successful routines). The next step is to identify the various desired responses that would be appropriate for the identified stimulus conditions (e.g., a range of teacher-provided prompts) and to contrast those responses with other potential undesired responses learners may make in similar conditions (e.g., last-minute lesson preparations). Finally, you'd want to select and explicitly train **examples** that sample the range of stimuli and responses within the identified stimulus and response classes (i.e., "Do this at this time") and help learners discriminate these from other **non-examples** of incorrect stimuli and/or responses (i.e., "Don't do this" and/or "Not at this time"). Figure 2.5 illustrates a range of examples for the stimulus class and response classes that would be important to consider when training teachers the skill of prompting. The black boxes also identify the non-examples of stimuli (S$^\Delta$) and responses to be used when selecting non-examples. Thus, general case programming allows you to establish stimulus control between a class of stimuli and a class of responses, finding an appropriate balance between discrimination and generalization.

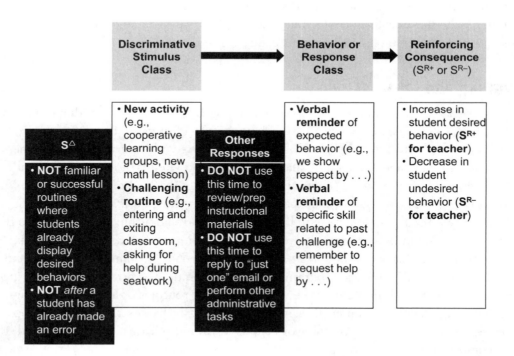

FIGURE 2.5. Example of training stimulus classes and response classes to promote generalization of one teacher behavior: the practice of delivering prompts and precorrections for expected student behavior.

Prompting

Last, but not least, we can use prompting to increase the likelihood that the trained S^{D}s occasion the desired responses. As you noticed, we used prompting as an example of teacher behavior (i.e., the practice of providing prompts to increase desired student behavior) throughout the last section, as prompting is an important classroom management practice. However, prompting is also an important strategy to increase teacher behavior.

Approaches to Prompting

There are a variety of ways to prompt, including verbal (e.g., providing explicit directions), gestural (e.g., pointing to something), visual (e.g., hanging a poster on a wall), and physical (e.g., using hand-over-hand to help a student with letter formation). Prompts can provide varying levels of information, from fully modeling (e.g., showing a successful demonstration of a behavior) or providing direct guidance (e.g., step-by-step directions) to providing indirect or minimal guidance (e.g., a hint about expected behavior).

When training teachers, we typically find that we start by modeling a classroom practice during training (described in more detail in Chapter 5), and we provide direct prompts in this context, too. For example, before asking teachers to script and practice specific praise statements, we may remind them about the critical features of specific praise. However, outside the training context, we often shift our mode of prompting to be less intensive. For example, after training, we may provide weekly emails to (1) remind teachers about the importance of specific praise, (2) highlight critical features, and (3) continue to provide a range of examples (and non-examples). We may also ask teachers to implement prompts for themselves (e.g., writing a few planned specific praise statements into their instructional materials), and we may intensify our approach if a teacher requires more support (e.g., providing verbal reminders via headphones, also known as "bug in ear," to cue teachers to use specific praise in the moment; Stumphauzer, 1971). We discuss training and prompting in greater detail in Chapters 5 and 6.

Guidelines for Effective Prompting

Regardless of the specific context, skill, or prompting approach, there are guidelines to increase the effectiveness of prompting. First, carefully select and plan prompts to promote success. We know that most learners (including teachers) will require additional prompting when a skill is new or difficult, and over time learners may require prompts to support maintenance (periodic reminders until the skill is fully maintained in the absence of outside support) and generalization (reminders about how a trained skill can be implemented and/ or adapted in new contexts). Second, provide the least amount of prompting necessary to ensure success. For example, we couldn't (and shouldn't) jump straight to providing bug-in-ear prompting for every teacher in the school. However, we could (and should) provide email reminders after training to encourage implementation of CWPBIS practices. Third, fade prompts as quickly as possible, while still ensuring learners' success. For example, if we have intensified prompting for a teacher (e.g., using bug-in-ear or a similarly intense strategy) based on a data-indicated need, we'd want to monitor the teacher's performance carefully. When data indicate that learners have met the goal we've set with them for practice implementation, we'd gradually reduce the frequency and intensity of our prompting until they are eventually implementing the practice effectively in their natural classroom environment (without our support). As these examples illustrate, prompts can be used in conjunction with other teaching strategies (e.g., shaping, chaining, general case programming), and we'll provide many more examples of how prompting can be used in the context of coaching in Chapter 6.

Reinforcing

We have already described types of reinforcement (positive and negative) and provided examples of how those are already present in the classroom setting and how reinforcement plays a role in shaping, chaining, establishing stimulus control, and general case programming. However, we would like to end this chapter with a reminder that increasing or decreasing the likelihood of any adult behavior can be difficult. The longer we've been practicing our current behaviors, the harder it can be to change. As we described for prompting, teachers will need more support (such as prompts and reinforcement) when skills are new and difficult. Therefore, coaching functions include not only teaching CWPBIS practices and providing prompts to promote implementation, but also celebrating (and hopefully reinforcing) successes. As we described in the section on shaping, those successes may be small and incremental, but success breeds success—and we want to increase the likelihood of future success through reinforcement.

A FEW FINAL THOUGHTS ABOUT THE SCIENCE OF BEHAVIOR

So, why does all of this matter, and what is it doing here? The reason is this: The mechanisms behind **how** behavior works will never change. Antecedents continuously change (e.g., think about how technology has changed in the last decade and the impact that has had on students and educators), behaviors change, and what students (and adults!) find reinforcing changes, but the mechanisms behind those concepts never do. Behavior followed by pleasant consequences will be repeated, no matter the behavior nor the consequences deemed pleasant by the learner. The science of behavior applies to **all** behavior, including social behaviors and academic behaviors, and to all those who behave.

SUMMARY

Whew! You've made it to the end of one of the longer chapters in our book, and (hopefully) you've learned (or reviewed) a lot about the behavioral principles that underlie all behavior, including the behavior of educators. You should now be able to describe the ABCs (or BCAs) of behavior and provide examples of how these concepts apply to critical teacher behaviors (i.e., implementation of CWPBIS practices), and you have begun to identify how you can use these principles to change (e.g., prompt, occasion, teach, reinforce) teachers' implementation of practices in the classroom context. We also suggest that you "think functionally" about errors (or the absence of them) in implementation. Continue to refer back to this chapter as you progress through the rest of this book, and use our phases of learning activities below to ensure that you are not just fluent but maintaining and generalizing your understanding of these principles.

PHASES OF LEARNING ACTIVITIES: CHAPTER 2

Acquisition

1. On a sheet of paper or in an electronic document, make yourself a glossary of the definitions of key behavioral concepts from this chapter. This will help you build fluency and will come in handy as you apply these concepts to what you learn while moving through the rest of the book.

2. Identify three tasks that you've completed in the last 48 hours (e.g., running an errand, making a phone call, even reading this chapter). Then, for each task, identify (using your newly acquired behavior notation, if you wish!) the antecedent, behavior, and consequence(s) associated with that task. What occasioned you engaging in the specific behavior? What consequence was present (or is normally present) that maintains this behavior? What, if anything, happened that may decrease the likelihood of you engaging in that behavior again in the future? Identify any relevant setting events that may have impacted the consequence value for a specific task.

Fluency

1. Review Figure 2.2 and "sketch out" (you don't need to draw, but a graphic organizer may help!) how a behavior in which you engage regularly (e.g., the route you take to work, the way you do laundry, the system you use to manage household finances) was learned through discrimination training and eventually brought under stimulus control. Use appropriate behavioral language (and notation, if you like) to describe the process.

2. Design a presentation (e.g., PowerPoint) that summarizes the content of this chapter in a way that would make it clear to your audience and set the stage for learning about supporting teachers' CWPBIS implementation. How would you explain these behavioral concepts—some of which are pretty complex—to a group who'd never heard them before?

Maintenance

1. Review a school discipline handbook from a local school (these are usually available on a school's website). What do you see that might align with the concept of "reinforcement" as presented in this chapter? What do you see that might align with the concept of "punishment"

as presented in this chapter? What about stimulus control? Reflect on what, if any, evidence of "thinking functionally" about student behavior appears in the school discipline handbook.

2. Now, review materials from a professional development training on a desired teacher behavior (academic or related to classroom management) that you've attended or led recently. What do you see in those materials that align with some of the behavioral approaches to teaching mentioned in this chapter? Is a modeling, shaping, or chaining process clearly detailed? How about prompting? Is there evidence of attention to the teachers' phase of learning embedded in the training materials? Use specific examples to support your answer.

Generalization

1. Review Figure 2.3, and then create two similar graphics with different teacher responses (i.e., CWPBIS practices) at the center (e.g., opportunity to respond, prompting for desired behavior). What would the antecedent and consequence possibilities be for the responses you've selected? Write a statement about stimulus control (i.e., how the different types of antecedent stimuli relate to the consequences) for each response you select.

2. Watch the evening news or read several articles about current news stories. Within this content, identify applications of behavioral theory to the stories and people featured. What antecedents occasion responses, and what consequences appear to be maintaining (or decreasing) the future likelihood of behavior? How do you know? What types of setting events do you see that impact the value of consequences for the people featured in the stories? Are there examples of extinction, or functional thinking? Although this may seem like a strange question, we promise it's a way to promote generalization of your knowledge of behavioral theory. Once you can successfully identify the mechanisms of behavior and begin to understand how behavior works, you'll see evidence of the science of behavior everywhere you look.

CHAPTER 3

Overview of Implementation Supports for Teachers

CHAPTER OBJECTIVES

By the end of this chapter, you should be able to . . .

1. Define implementation based on current research-supported models.
2. Describe the critical features of PBIS (i.e., outcomes, data, practices, and systems).
3. Discuss how to organize systems of support for teachers within a PBIS framework.

Imagine This: *You are a member of your school's PBIS team. Your team has begun working with staff and students to implement evidence-based practices within the PBIS framework, and your initial results are promising. You've seen a decrease in office discipline referrals, and you've heard staff talking about how much better behavior is in the hallways and cafeteria. As you walk through the office patting yourself on the back, you overhear a school administrator complaining about implementation within one of the grade levels in your building. You hear the administrator say, "I'll be sure to address those teachers' poor implementation in their upcoming evaluations!" You realize that your team's initial efforts have primarily focused on supports for students and that the approach for staff members is still fairly reactive and punitive. You start to think there must be a better way. Shouldn't educators also benefit from a positive and proactive environment? Can PBIS be implemented for educators, too?*

OVERVIEW OF IMPLEMENTATION SUPPORTS

We strongly believe that educators can do their best work when school and district leaders invest in positive and proactive supports. The PBIS framework can (and should!) be used to organize supports for educators. As you read in the last chapter, behavioral principles apply to everyone. Our goal is to apply behavioral principles to set educators up for success, provide ongoing support to all educators, intensify supports based on data, and celebrate successes. To do that, we need to have a better understanding of how to arrange environments and promote implementation at an organizational (e.g., school and district) level. In this chapter, we (1) provide an overview of implementation, focusing on implementation phases and drivers, (2) summarize recommendations for supporting implementation, and (3) describe the critical features of the PBIS framework, with an emphasis of developing systems to support educators.

Implementation Phases

As you have likely experienced, implementation is not an "all-or-nothing" endeavor, nor is it always a smooth and linear process. Instead, implementation progresses in much the same way as the process of learning to walk. Initially, we practice walking while someone holds our hands and provides the support we need to stay vertical. Then, as we start to walk on our own, we may initially take one step before we fall and need help to get up. Next, we may take a few wobbly steps forward, stumble backward, fall, and cry. Over time, we continue to build upon our initial steps and increase our ability and comfort with walking. Before long, walking just becomes the way we move from place to place—without even thinking about it, it's the way we move forward.

Like walking, implementation progresses through several stages or phases, and we may move backward before we move forward. When we are fully implementing, it just becomes what we do—without even thinking about it, it's the way we move forward. Fixsen, Blase, Naoom, and Duda (2013) at the National Implementation Research Network (NIRN) have spent years studying research and processes related to implementation within organizations, including schools and districts. They have suggested that there are key phases of implementation: exploration, installation, initial implementation, and full implementation. The NIRN has developed resources to support implementation in their AI Hub, a comprehensive resource providing additional guidance, detail, and examples of the phases of implementation described in the next paragraphs.

Exploration

During the exploration phase, educators examine data to determine whether there is a need for change. If a need is established, educators (1) identify potential practices, innovations, or adaptations that are aligned with the need for change; (2) explore the resources and processes involved with implementation to explore contextual fit; and (3) select an appropriate practice, innovation, or adaptation. Finally, educators seek and build support from a variety of stakeholders to move toward implementation.

For example, educational leaders within one district may examine their discipline data and notice that their overall rates of office discipline referrals (ODRs) are increasing relative to previous years. Within their district, teachers may be raising concerns about student behavior with administrators and union representatives, and administrators may observe teachers increasingly taking days off or even leaving their district. Therefore, the district leaders may identify a need for a districtwide approach to both decreasing students' challenging behavior and increasing supports for teachers. District leaders may meet with state-level consultants, explore approaches implemented by model districts within their state or region, examine approaches that are considered evidence based, or combine some of these approaches to identify possible practices, innovations, or adaptations to their current district practices for supporting students and teachers. During this process, the district leaders may realize that their state supports PBIS (e.g., by offering grants to schools interested in implementing PBIS), find model districts implementing PBIS in their state, and learn that PBIS is an empirically supported framework for delivering evidence-based practices. As they learn more, the district leaders may find out that PBIS is designed to be adapted to the local culture and context, and they may decide to apply for an available grant to support their schools' exploration of PBIS. As the district leaders apply for the grant, they begin to communicate the benefits of PBIS to educators and family members in their schools, present their plans for implementing PBIS to their school boards, and start a "whisper campaign" among students to build interest. These steps begin to generate stakeholder support for the next phase of implementation.

Installation

Installation is the process of planning for implementation. During the installation phase, educators secure resources, training, and other implementation supports necessary to implement the selected practice, innovation, or adaptation in the future. Educators use the installation phase to develop the systems needed to support implementation, including developing processes for communicating, reviewing data, obtaining feedback, and making decisions to support and adjust implementation across time. In other words, educators build the structures and develop detailed plans to enable the future implementation of their selected practice, innovation, or adaptation.

For example, after learning that they have received a small grant to support PBIS in their district, district leaders identify a representative team from each school (e.g., an administrator, a representative group of educators and noncertified staff, one or two family members, and at least one student) and their district (e.g., district administrators with expertise in data, behavior, and related topics) to attend a state-sponsored team training series on PBIS. From each team, the district leaders may identify two team members to function as coaches, who will attend an additional coaches' training series. During the team and coach training series, the teams and coaches (1) learn about the critical features of the PBIS framework; (2) develop an action plan to guide their contextualized implementation of evidence-based practices within a PBIS framework; (3) draft examples of products (e.g., expectations matrix, lesson plans, student and staff recognition systems); (4) include a plan to train staff and recruit feedback as part of their action plan; and (5) begin to secure resources (e.g., time on the professional development calendar, data systems, time for coaching functions) necessary for implementation the following year. PBIS teams typically spend 1 full year in the installation phase while participating in training and receiving ongoing support for their installation activities.

Initial Implementation

During the initial implementation phase, educators begin to implement the selected practice, innovation, or adaptation. Implementation supports during this phase, including ongoing training, coaching, and feedback, focus on accurate implementation (i.e., initial acquisition) and increasing fluency with implementation. If this language reminds you of the phases of learning (from Chapter 1), you're right on track!

For example, a school-based PBIS leadership team may implement their professional development (PD) plan, introducing the full "rollout" of PBIS to their staff during the beginning-of-school PD days. During a PBIS training, team members may share the expectations matrix and lesson plans developed with staff input the previous spring, show a video model of how to teach one lesson (e.g., being respectful in the hallway), and describe their plan to use a "passport" to track students' progress (by class) through various instructional stations set up during the first week of school to that ensure all students are taught how to engage in expected behavior in every school setting. Then, staff members implement the plan, delivering social skills instruction in expected behavior within each school setting, and they "catch" students engaging in behavior that meets or exceeds the school expectations. When "catching" students, staff members tell students exactly what the students did well (i.e., specific praise) and provide a "positive referral" that students can use to buy privileges (e.g., choosing music to listen to, passing out material) in their classroom. At monthly PBIS leadership team meetings, the team reviews academic, behavioral (i.e., office and positive referrals), and other screening data to monitor and adjust PBIS implementation, to identify students who may require additional support to be successful, and to offer support to staff members whose data indicate implementation challenges. Throughout the year, the PBIS leadership team and coaches continue to attend training events to refine their practices, including enhancing family engagement, focusing on equity, and shoring up implementation in their classrooms. At the end of the year, the PBIS leadership team works with a district-based coach to complete the Tiered Fidelity Inventory (TFI; Algozzine et al., 2014) to assess their overall fidelity of implementation and use all collected data to update their action plan and adjust implementation for the next year.

Full Implementation

During full implementation, educators are consistently implementing the selected practice, innovation, or adaptation, with minimal external support. In other words, the local (i.e., district- and school-based) leaders have developed internal capacity to support implementation. The leadership team can use its established implementation framework to adapt their implementation supports and practices, as needed, to meet new or changing needs indicated by the data. In other words, the implemented practice, innovation, or adaptation has become the team's "way of work," and its members can nimbly adjust to meet ongoing needs. In the language of the phases of learning, the team has been able to maintain and generalize their implementation.

For example, 5 years after initial PBIS implementation, the leadership team from a particular school has experienced some turnover. There is a new administrator, a few new teachers, a new parent (as the previous parent's student graduated), and feedback from new students. The team has maintained the same core expectations, but they continue to update and refine how they teach those expectations across the school context. They no longer use a paper passport but instead use iPads to track each student's initial instruction on each expectation within each setting/routine. The team has also refined the recognition system, allowing students to use tickets to buy needed school supplies, purchase tickets to school events, or donate tickets (i.e., convert tickets to money raised by the school's parent–teacher organization) to local emergency funds (e.g., a hurricane relief effort to support a coastal city in their state). Team members continue to meet monthly and review data, using a planned agenda; however, their meetings have become shorter and more efficient, leaving room for the team to increase the scope of their agenda to include integration and alignment with other district or state initiatives (e.g., social–emotional competence, restorative practices). Each year, the team continues to complete the TFI, but they now use TFI data to evaluate their implementation in terms of supporting all needs for all students. Furthermore, the team realizes that they no longer refer to what they're doing as PBIS, even though their implementation is still true to the PBIS core features. Instead, the system they have built has just become their school's way of doing business. The expectations are depicted in murals around the school, the students know that the expectations will be taught at the beginning of the year and again in the spring, and families know to ask students about their day (including tickets earned for exceeding expectations).

Implementation Drivers

In addition to considering phases of implementation, the group at the NIRN has studied elements that facilitate, or drive, implementation (Fixsen, Blase, Duda, Naoom, & Van Dyke, 2010). Specifically, Fixsen, Blase, and colleagues (Fixsen et al., 2010, 2013) have identified and described leadership, organizational, and competency drivers.

Leadership Drivers

Leadership drivers include the technical and adaptive skills required to facilitate implementation of a new practice or, in the case of PBIS, a framework within a school, district, or state. Fixsen and colleagues describe leadership as neither a title nor a person, but behaviors in which individuals within an organization engage to promote and sustain effective programming over time. Therefore, we certainly hope that administrators engage in leadership behaviors, but we can also look to other formal (e.g., mentors, staff with specialized training and skills) or informal (e.g., teachers with social influence, administrative staff with the pulse of the school) leaders to support change. Furthermore, Fixsen and colleagues indicate that "adaptive" or flexible leadership behaviors are necessary in the early phases of implementation but that technical leadership skills (e.g., data-based decision making) are required to sustain implementation within an organization. For example, a visionary school administrator may effectively argue the need for a schoolwide approach to supporting student and staff behavior, and she may see opportunities to leverage existing resources creatively in order to develop a leadership team and secure training for her staff (i.e., she has demonstrated flexible leadership). However, as the leadership team begins participating in training, they will need support from a leader who, first, understands how to develop and use data systems and, second, has the behavioral expertise to support the implementation of practices and systems (i.e., a leader with technical leadership skills).

Organizational Drivers

Organizational drivers create supportive host environments in which staff can implement practices. These drivers include systems intervention, facilitative leadership, and a system to support data-based decision making. For example, a school or district implementing PBIS may ensure that administrators (1) facilitate implementation through their priorities, which are communicated through clear policies supporting implementation, (2) ensure that resources are available to support implementation, and (3) make data-based decisions that are clearly communicated to all stakeholders.

Competency Drivers

Competency drivers support the ability of staff to implement selected practices with fidelity. Specifically, staff selection, training, and coaching are three of the strategies that can be implemented at the organizational (i.e., school and district) level to promote staff competency. First, being able to recruit and hire staff members who have appropriate prerequisite skills enables an organization to maximize the likelihood of successful implementation. When implementing PBIS, for example, hiring educators with a background in positive behavioral support practices or at least an interest in a proactive, rather than reactive, approach to behavior would be a strength. Second, providing comprehensive PD for newly hired and existing staff members (as we discuss in Part II of this book) is critical to acquiring skills required for successful implementation. Finally, although training is necessary for acquiring skills, ongoing coaching with data-based performance feedback (as we discuss in Chapter 7) is necessary to promote high fidelity of implementation at a level that enables staff to maintain and adapt their implementation across contexts.

In sum, Fixsen, Blase, and their colleagues at the NIRN have demonstrated that implementation "develops" in phases. Although we provided examples to demonstrate how overall implementation of SWPBIS may evolve from exploration to full implementation, the timelines for implementation of specific practices may be more varied. For example, teaching and reinforcing expected behavior within nonclassroom settings may be part of initial PBIS implementation in a school, whereas a leadership team may still be developing plans to install practices within classroom settings. Thus, it is critical that school and district leadership teams invest in implementation drivers to support implementation of all selected practices across various phases of implementation. Although this may seem like a daunting task, we have found that existing structures within the PBIS framework already set schools up for success with careful consideration of phases and drivers of implementation.

USING PBIS TO ORGANIZE SUPPORTS FOR TEACHERS: BUILDING SYSTEMS OF SUPPORT

In Chapter 1, we provided a brief overview of the critical elements of PBIS: **data** to drive decision making, **practices** to support students, **systems** to support staff, and locally meaningful **outcomes**. In this section, we revisit each critical feature, with a more intentional focus on the outcomes, data, and systems components of staff implementation of PBIS in the classroom. We also link the implementation drivers to these PBIS elements, illustrating how fully investing in a PBIS framework supports effective implementation of evidence-based practices across all school settings, especially classrooms.

Practices

Practices are the specific strategies educators implement in their classrooms to support students' behavior, including (1) thoughtfully designing the physical layout of the classroom; (2) establishing and teaching routines; (3) selecting, defining, and teaching positively stated expectations in the context of classroom routines; (4) actively engaging students with instruction; (5) providing specific feedback (i.e., praise and corrections) contingent on student behavior; and (6) implementing a continuum of consequence strategies to acknowledge appropriate behavior and respond to inappropriate behavior. If you'd like a more in-depth review of these practices than provided in Chapter 1, we suggest you read the companion to this book, as these practices are described in great detail in Simonsen and Myers (2015). The goal for educators is to implement classroom practices with sufficient intensity and fidelity so most (> 80%) students experience improved outcomes.

Outcomes

As we described in Chapter 1, outcomes should be locally determined, meaningful, observable, measurable, specific, and achievable. District and school leadership teams develop outcomes to measure the effects of PBIS implementation on all students. In addition, each teacher identifies specific goals for his or her implementation of classroom practices, specifying desired improvements in student outcomes. For example, a teacher may specify that PBIS practices are implemented with sufficient fidelity if 80% of students are able to demonstrate expected behavior during 80% of sampled opportunities in the classroom.

Although the ultimate goal of PBIS implementation is improving student outcomes, outcomes for staff are critical for successful implementation and accountability. For example, school leadership teams may develop an overall outcome for fidelity of implementation (e.g.,

"Given training and coaching supports, school staff will implement the PBIS framework with fidelity as measured by achieving a 70% on the TFI"). Alternately, a school leadership team may want to identify specific outcomes related to their implementation (e.g., "With supports from the schoolwide leadership team, at least 80% of educators will give at least four positive referrals for every office discipline referral"). By including outcomes focused on staff implementation, school and district leadership teams hold themselves accountable (i.e., teams detail how they will support staff and how those efforts will be measured) for providing sufficient supports to ensure effective implementation.

Data

Once outcomes are identified for students and staff, school and district leadership teams collect data on indicators of student behavior and related outcomes (e.g., academic performance, social and emotional competence) and staff implementation fidelity. Furthermore, just as we can't examine students' responsiveness to an intervention they haven't received (or to an intervention that's not implemented with sufficient fidelity), we can't examine educators' ability to effectively implement interventions (i.e., adult behavior) until we ensure that they have been provided with sufficient training, coaching, and performance feedback. Therefore, school and leadership teams also need to consider their fidelity of implementation of systems of support for staff. School and district leadership teams need a plan to collect data on (1) their fidelity of implementation of educator supports, (2) educators' fidelity of implementation of school and classroom practices, and (3) student outcomes. To enable this level of data-based decision making, leadership teams need organized data systems that allow team members to quickly enter information, efficiently generate graphs, and frequently monitor fidelity and outcomes. For schoolwide data, systems exist to monitor students' office discipline referrals (e.g., schoolwide information system [SWIS]; May et al., 2010), attendance (e.g., *eduphoria.net*), and academic skills (e.g., Dynamic Indicators of Basic Early Literacy Skills [DIBELS]; Dynamic Measurement Group, 2008); to screen for students who may need more support to develop their social and emotional competence (e.g., Social Skills Intervention System; Gresham & Elliot, 2008); and to monitor schoolwide fidelity of implementation (e.g., *pbis.assessment.org*).

Alone, these systems may not be sensitive enough to monitor students' classroom behavior, teachers' implementation of classroom practices, or leadership teams' implementation of staff supports. To supplement these broader systems of data collection, Swain-Bradway and colleagues (2017) developed a guide to support data-based decision making related to classroom practices and systems. In particular, Swain-Bradway and colleagues proposed a decision-making cycle that begins with fidelity of implementation of staff support systems (i.e., training, coaching, and performance feedback) or classroom practices, depending on whether the team is monitoring fidelity and outcomes for staff or students, respectively (see Figure 3.1). After determining that supports are being implemented with fidelity, they suggest examining outcomes to determine whether staff members or students are responding to supports. In the event that not all staff members or students are responding, Swain-

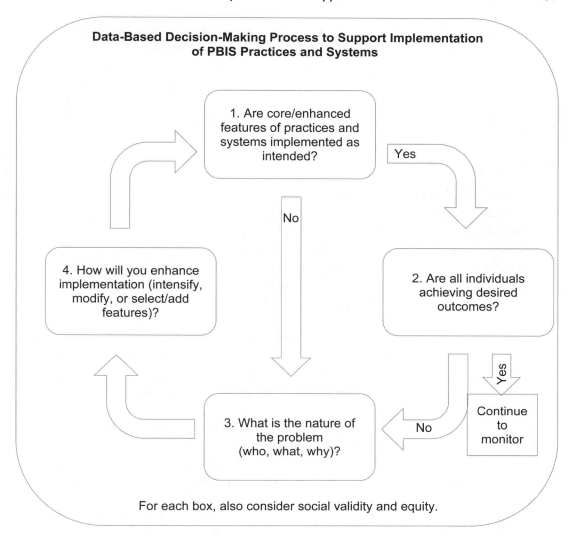

FIGURE 3.1. This cycle illustrates how (1) individual educators can evaluate and make decisions to enhance their implementation of PBIS practices and (2) school leadership teams can evaluate and make decisions to enhance PD support systems for educators in a building. This figure was developed by members of the Office of Special Education Technical Assistance Center on PBIS and was previously published in Simonsen et al. (2019). Copyright 2019 by West Virginia University Press. Reprinted by permission.

Bradway and colleagues propose engaging in a problem-solving process to determine who is not responding and to precisely define the problem, including aspects of the context that may be contributing, based on data. Lastly, they recommend developing an action plan to guide implementation of a targeted solution and monitoring implementation and outcomes of their action plan. By effectively using data to guide and monitor implementation, leadership teams can increase the likelihood that students (and staff!) benefit.

Systems

At the center of all of these elements are the systems that support staff. Although we have described the systems that support educators' implementation of SWPBIS (e.g., a representative leadership team with identified coaches, a plan for overall PD, staff recognition) in Chapter 1, we find that these supports are rarely sufficiently focused or intensive enough to promote effective, efficient, and durable implementation of CWPBIS practices. Therefore, school and district leadership teams need to invest in systems features that are focused on educators' implementation of CWPBIS.

School and district leadership teams need to develop an overall PD approach that incorporates training, coaching, and feedback for all instructional and behavioral support practices. First, leadership teams need to establish their system's foundations, which include priority, resources, and integration and alignment with existing PD approaches and practices. These systems elements are aligned with Fixsen and colleagues' concept of "organizational drivers."

Second, leadership teams need to engage in positive and proactive PD supports. Freeman, Simonsen, and colleagues (2017) further defined critical features of PD supports for educators, indicating that successful training includes an effective model or demonstration of the practice, examples and non-examples of implementation, and opportunities for staff to try implementing the practice in the training context while receiving feedback (similar to the best practices we enact with our K–12 students!). Effective coaching includes antecedent prompts, or reminders, of critical elements of the trained practice(s). Although coaching may include low-intensity supports (e.g., email reminders sent to all staff), coaching can also be intensified based on teams' needs to include intensive, individualized, and *in vivo* supports (e.g., *in vivo* modeling, bug-in-ear prompting). Furthermore, coaching must be supplemented with data-based performance feedback that enables educators to see their performance in the context of their past performance and a criterion (e.g., goal for implementation) so educators can receive positive feedback when their performance meets or exceeds the criterion and supportive corrective feedback with specific suggestions for improvement. These PD supports are parallel to Fixsen and colleagues' "capacity drivers."

In addition to effective PD supports, school and district leadership teams need to ensure that they have an effective staff recognition or acknowledgment system that can be used to recognize (and reinforce!) educators' effective implementation of classroom PBIS practices. Furthermore, this system may also be used to recognize school and district leaders who provide effective training, coaching, and performance feedback supports. Ensuring that staff members are recognized for their efforts toward implementation will promote a supportive and positive staff culture that will enable the remaining PD supports to be implemented effectively. As with developing any recognition system, leadership teams need to (1) identify the implementation behaviors they want to increase, (2) determine how they will recognize the identified behaviors, and (3) monitor the system to ensure that it is functioning to increase (i.e., reinforce) implementation and not leading to negative side effects (e.g., negative stigma, unhealthy competition among staff). For example, one school wanted to increase staff members' positive communications with students, relative to corrective feedback. The PBIS leadership team decided to recognize the staff members who provided the most tickets to students, paired with specific feedback. To determine how to recognize behaviors, team members surveyed staff members to determine preferred types of items and activities. Many staff members indicated that they would want to either arrive late or get out of school early (i.e., "G.O.O.S.E."). Based on these data, the team purchased an old (and so-ugly-it-was-cute) goose stuffed animal and "awarded" it to the teacher who distributed the highest number of tickets in a given week. During the following week (while the goose "lived" in that classroom), the teacher could choose one morning to arrive late or one afternoon to leave early, and a PBIS team member would provide coverage. Each week, the goose traveled to a new classroom, based on data indicating the teacher who distributed the most tickets. In future months, the leadership team realized that the goose could be used to recognize other desired staff behaviors (e.g., effective lesson planning, positive parent contacts, implementing an effective warmup routine), so they moved to randomly selecting a staff behavior each week to encourage staff members to be at their best over time. (Does this remind you of the maintenance and generalization phases of learning? It should!) By implementing a recognition system, this school reinforced (i.e., increased) the staff implementation behaviors they valued—behaviors that resulted in better outcomes for students—and they also contributed to a positive staff culture, which supported their ongoing efforts to improve classroom practices.

WHAT DOES THIS MEAN FOR CWPBIS?

Although the first sections of this chapter primarily illustrate implementation with *schoolwide* PBIS examples, we want to emphasize that the same phases of implementation, the same implementation drivers, and the same critical elements driving SWPBIS apply to CWPBIS. In the best-case scenario, educators are working to implement CWPBIS in a school that already has an SWPBIS system in place; everyone speaks the same "language," all stakeholders understand a proactive and positive approach to behavior support, and some practices (e.g., token economies) at the schoolwide level can be adapted and implemented at the classwide level. As mentioned above, even in schools and districts in which SWPBIS is implemented with fidelity, a structured approach to support teachers' implementation of CWPBIS is needed. The "Systems" section describes what that can look like.

You may be asking, "What if I work in a school or district that isn't implementing PBIS at the schoolwide level?" You may even be working in a school that does not embrace a scientifically based approach to behavior. First of all, great work thinking about how to implement CWPBIS on your own. If you are taking your PD into your own hands, we suggest that you review Chapter 1 extensively and immerse yourself in some of the resources we suggested. Search *www.pbis.org* for additional resources and attend relevant webinars and conferences offered through various PD organizations (e.g., the Association for Positive Behavior Support). Contact your local university about relevant classes or workshops you could attend (or look for online courses you may be able to take), and be sure to talk to your administration about potentially supporting these opportunities. It may not be easy, but we promise that you'll find the results—which can include improved student behavior, a more efficiently run classroom, and a more positive attitude about your class and profession— highly reinforcing.

SUMMARY

In this chapter, we (1) summarized implementation phases and drivers, based on the work of Fixsen, Blase, and colleagues at the NIRN; (2) described the critical elements of PBIS with a focus on staff implementation of classroom PBIS practices; and (3) demonstrated how the PBIS framework aligns with the implementation work of the NIRN. In the rest of this book, we provide an overview of PD models (Chapter 4) and detailed discussion (Chapters 5–8) of systems to support educators' implementation of classroom practices.

PHASES OF LEARNING ACTIVITIES: CHAPTER 3

Acquisition

1. Identify each of the four key phases of implementation within organizations and provide a brief definition of each.
2. Identify each of the three types of implementation drivers that facilitate implementation and proved a brief definition of each.

Fluency

1. Create a graphic organizer representing the four core elements of PBIS (i.e., outcomes, systems, data, and practices). This graphic organizer should demonstrate how the elements work together and include examples of what each element might look like when designing implementation supports for teachers.
2. Develop a checklist for school administrators who are interested in providing implementation support to their school staff, many of whom are new to PBIS. What would administrators need to do to ensure that they are supporting the PBIS team with the phases of implementation and those elements driving the implementation?

Maintenance

1. Describe how the four key phases of implementation align with the four phases of learning and provide specific school-based examples demonstrating how the two models work together.

2. Design a PowerPoint or other type of presentation that you would use to introduce the concept of implementation supports to the faculty at a school that is beginning their SWPBIS implementation. This presentation should detail specific activities undertaken by the PBIS team and expectations for school staff.

Generalization

1. Think about your school or classroom. By yourself or in conjunction with colleagues (if you're able), use Figure 3.1 as a map for designing your own data-based decision-making process with specific examples applicable to your context. What are the specific questions that you would ask as you evaluate your progress toward the outcomes you've identified? Draft an action plan (as required in Step 4) based on what you learn.

2. Review the phases of implementation, implementation drivers, and the data-based decision-making process (i.e., Figure 3.1). Describe what the application of implementation supports would look like in a nonschool setting (e.g., business, government). What aspects of implementation would be similar to implementation in a school setting? What would be different? What might schools learn from implementation efforts in other sectors?

PART II

Empirically Supported Strategies to Support Teachers' Classwide PBIS Implementation

CHAPTER 4

A Road Map to Building Systems of Support for Teachers

Imagine This: *You were hired as a district-level behavior coach for a district that has been implementing SWPBIS for more than 5 years. Despite generally strong overall implementation (i.e., fidelity scores meeting the criterion), the district administrators have told you that your main focus is to support teachers with their implementation of CWPBIS. What sounded like an exciting opportunity during your job interview now feels like a daunting task. It's the beginning of the summer, and you have approximately 2 months to design a comprehensive PD approach for all of the teachers in your district. Before getting started, grab a cup of coffee, tea, water, or your beverage of choice and dive into this chapter for a quick overview of how to approach designing a PD system to support teachers' CWPBIS implementation.*

SUPPORTING TEACHERS' CWPBIS IMPLEMENTATION

In this section of the book, we explore specific ways to support teachers, and this chapter sets the stage by providing an overview or road map to help you build a system of support for teachers in your school, district, or organization. Before we discuss different ways to support teachers' CWPBIS implementation in subsequent chapters, we want to use this chapter to review common definitions and guiding principles related to systems of support, provide an overview of common approaches to PD, describe how these approaches relate to the behavioral principles you have already learned, and give you a way to organize all of this information in a simple action plan. Let's start by getting on the same page with common definitions!

Common Definitions

Darling-Hammond, Hyler, and Gardner (2017) "define effective **professional development** [PD] as structured professional learning that results in changes to teacher knowledge and practices, and improvements in student learning outcomes" (p. 2, emphasis added). Furthermore, they "conceptualize **professional learning** as a product of both externally provided and job-embedded activities that increase teachers' knowledge and help them change their instructional practice in ways that support student learning" (p. 2, emphasis added). We agree: PD is how we achieve professional learning.

Several key strategies are typically employed as components of a comprehensive PD system or framework: training, coaching, mentoring, performance feedback, and self-management. We describe each of these approaches in detail in subsequent chapters. For now, we want to provide brief definitions, as these approaches may be used and described in a variety of ways.

First, **training** includes explicit instruction in one or more classroom practices (e.g., opportunities to respond, specific praise). Training typically includes (1) an effective *model*, or demonstration, of the practice, (2) an opportunity to engage in guided practice alongside other teachers during the training (*lead*), and (3) a brief assessment of teachers' knowledge and application during the training (e.g., independent practice, *test*) with feedback.

Following training, most effective PD models incorporate coaching. In their meta-analysis, Kraft, Blazar, and Hogan (2018) defined **coaching** as activities in which "coaches or peers observe teachers' instruction and provide feedback to help them improve" and clarified that "coaching is intended to be individualized, time-intensive, sustained over the course of a semester or year, context specific, and focused on discrete skills" (p. 2). When coaching or consultation is provided by an identified mentor as part of an ongoing relationship, these practices are typically described as **mentoring**; however, mentoring may have a broader set of functions (e.g., managing work–life balance) than coaching (Kraft et al., 2018).

In PBIS, **coaching** is defined by a set of functions including (1) antecedent strategies such as providing prompts (e.g., verbally reminding, modeling) and rearranging the environment to support practice implementation and (2) consequence strategies, such as providing specific, data-based feedback on practice implementation (Freeman, Sugai, Simonsen, & Everett, 2017). Thus, data-based performance feedback is a critical component of coaching and mentoring.

Performance feedback involves monitoring and providing data-based graphic feedback on one or more target behaviors (e.g., specific praise rate; Noell et al., 2005). Because we consider coaching and performance feedback as two separate but related components of a comprehensive PD system, we consistently use the term "coaching" to describe antecedent strategies (e.g., prompting, arranging the environment) and the term "performance feedback" to describe consequence strategies (e.g., delivering data-based feedback, problem solving any challenges that arise, celebrating successes).

Finally, when teachers perform components of training, coaching, and performance feedback for themselves, these behaviors are known as self-management. **Self-management** occurs when an individual implements antecedent (e.g., self-delivered prompts), behavior (e.g., self-instruction, self-evaluation), and consequence (e.g., self-reinforcement) strategies to manage his or her own behavior (Skinner, 1953).

Now that we have common definitions for PD and typical approaches to supporting teachers, let's discuss the principles that should guide your selection of approaches to support teachers.

Guiding Principles

Regardless of the specific strategies or features you plan to include in your comprehensive system of support for teachers, there are several principles that should guide your selection, implementation, evaluation, and adaptation of systems. In particular, consider developing systems that are supportive, contextually and culturally relevant, sustained and sustainable, and research-based.

Supportive

First, supports should be *supportive*. That may sound redundant—how would supports *not* be supportive? However, we often hear stories of teachers feeling embarrassed to ask for help or being punished (e.g., given poor evaluations, provided negative feedback) if they struggle to implement CWPBIS. Given these stories, teachers may be concerned that supports (e.g., coaching, performance feedback) will be evaluative in nature or result in some negative or punitive outcome. Therefore, school leaders will need to (1) communicate positive and high expectations for CWPBIS implementation, (2) ensure that supports are positive and proactive (rather than reactive or evaluative), (3) deliver universal supports to all teachers to set them up for success, (4) provide additional differentiated support to ensure that all teachers are able to successfully meet the high expectations, and (5) promote a positively reinforcing staff culture. That is, when staff approach and meet the positive and high expectations, there should be opportunities to celebrate successes!

For example, a school leadership team may kick off the first back-to-school PD day with a statement about the district's and school's commitment to implementing SWPBIS to promote a positive school climate and desired outcomes for all students, and team members may announce that this year's emphasis is on ensuring that CWPBIS is implemented with fidelity in all classrooms (i.e., **positive and high expectations for implementation**). Then the leadership team may introduce their school's system of support for teachers, including brief trainings (at existing faculty meetings) and ongoing support from two CWPBIS "coaches" (i.e., **universal support**). The team introduces the two coaches, a school psychologist and a special educator, whose backgrounds in nonsupervisory behavioral roles make them ideally suited to help their peers. Furthermore, the team clarifies that the coaches' role is solely to support teachers and that any observations or information collected by coaches will be solely for the purpose of helping the teachers (i.e., **proactive and positive support**) and will not be shared with administrators. For teachers who may need more support, the team promises that coaches will be available for more intensive consultation and other supports, communicating that every teacher will get what he or she needs to be successful (i.e., **differentiated support**). By differentiating supports based on data, school leaders demonstrate respect for teachers' time, prior learning, skills, and expertise. Finally, the team may present their plan for sharing and celebrating successes, as teachers individually and collectively work toward effective CWPBIS implementation (i.e., **positively reinforcing climate and culture**).

Contextually and Culturally Relevant

In addition to making sure that supports are, in fact, supportive, it's critical that both the practices and systems are contextually and culturally relevant. As we described in Chapters 1 and 3, there are critical features of CWPBIS practices and systems to support teachers that should be present to set your school and district up for success. However, how those practices and systems are implemented should vary based on the cultural and contextual variables of your setting. For example, think about your school culture and climate when considering how to approach developing systems to support teachers. Is your environment positive, supportive, and collaborative? Or does your school have a history of "unsupportive supports"? Do teachers have a history of collecting and examining data on their own practices? Or does data-based performance feedback represent a significant break with past practice? Do most teachers already implement CWPBIS practices with sufficient fidelity to support most students? Or are many teachers struggling with CWPBIS basics? Each of these questions may guide you to a different choice for how you approach training, what practices you train, and how you will provide ongoing coaching and performance feedback.

　　If you're wondering how to measure the culture and climate of your school, we have some suggestions (and we commend you on your data-driven approach to supporting teachers!). It may be a good idea to begin with a review of school policies and procedures. Are they written in an inclusive fashion, incorporating all students and families? Are they available in all languages spoken by students and families in the school? Do they acknowledge and emphasize respect and consideration for students and families from all backgrounds, including cultures, races, ethnicities, socioeconomic status, religion (or lack thereof), sexual orientation, and ability levels? Are the mission and stated values of the school inclusive of all students and families? Are any procedures written in supportive (i.e., what *to* do) rather than punitive (i.e., what *not* to do) language? In addition, consider interviewing stakeholders who can provide additional information about the school's culture and climate. This includes students, staff members (think about what the cafeteria workers could share, for example), teachers, administrators, families, and community members. Schools and districts often have advisory councils made up of internal and external stakeholders; this body could provide a wealth of information about the culture and climate of a school or district.

There are also more structured approaches for gathering data about a school or district culture and climate. For example, schools can conduct a resource mapping exercise (e.g., Lever et al., 2014) to identify and organize resources available at the school and community levels. These resources can then be linked with the school's vision and goals to provide the most support and appropriate choices for students and their families. In addition, there are a number of school climate surveys, including:

- School Climate Survey (LaSalle, McIntosh, & Eliason, 2018).
- School Safety Survey (Sprague, Colvin, & Irvin, 2003).
- ED School Climate Surveys (EDSCLS; U.S. Department of Education, 2019).

Sustained and Sustainable

When building systems of support for teachers, the metaphor about it being a marathon, rather than a sprint, seems appropriate. Although traditional PD has often employed a one-shot, sit-and-get inservice model (Yoon, Duncan, Lee, Scarloss, & Shapley, 2007), decades of research demonstrate that this "sprint" to the PD finish does not result in a change in teacher practice (Fixsen, Naoom, Blase, Friedman, & Wallace, 2005; Joyce & Showers, 2002; Oliver & Reschly, 2007; Stokes & Baer, 1977). Instead, teachers' implementation does improve when training is supplemented with a "marathon" of ongoing, sustained coaching and performance feedback (e.g., Jeffrey, McCurdy, Ewing, & Polis, 2009; Simonsen, Myers, & DeLuca, 2010). Therefore, PD supports should be a sustained, long-term effort.

Just as PD should be sustained, it should also be sustain*able*. Research may support a "gold standard" approach that involves ongoing expert coaching and feedback, but it is unlikely that this intensive approach can be maintained in the absence of external support and funding. So, as you get excited about designing a new PD system for your school, you may be tempted to advocate for an impressive and intensive (and expensive!) level of support. However, be sure to keep your actual resources and constraints in mind, as many PD functions can be met in less resource-intensive ways. For example, our research suggests that teachers can efficiently and effectively perform many functions of coaching and performance feedback to improve their own implementation of classroom practices (e.g., Simonsen et al., 2017).

We explore these functions (i.e., coaching and performance feedback) in depth in Chapters 6 and 7, respectively, and we encourage you to read those chapters (and all chapters) with a focus on building capacity. That is, once training is over and supports are faded, how do we know that these practices will be maintained over time? How will they be sustained? If teachers can be trained how to apply coaching and performance feedback supports to their own practice, the likelihood of sustaining those practices increases dramatically. Remember our earlier discussion (in Chapter 2) about stimulus control? It's critical that teachers are under appropriate stimulus control; that is, the classroom itself should be the

S^D for reflective PBIS practices rather than an outside trainer or prompt from an administrator. Teachers must be able to assess their own strengths and weaknesses, collect data on their own performance, and use those data to make instructional and behavioral support decisions. For an in-depth discussion of how this can be accomplished, see Simonsen and Myers (2015).

Research-Based

A final guiding principle is to select PD supports that are likely to be effective, given your local context. In other words, consider supports that are research-based. When selecting PD supports, implementers should determine whether the PD has strong research demonstrating its effectiveness; that is, have studies shown that after the PD, outcomes for educators and students improve? Simply enjoying a PD session does not mean that educators will put what they've learned into practice or that what they've learned will translate into improved outcomes for students. Sustainability requires continued attention to and maintenance of all aspects of a system, including constant evaluation and changes based on collected data (Wallace, Blase, Fixsen, & Naoom, 2008). Although implementing a new practice or program is recursive and may take several years to achieve, sustainability should always be the ultimate goal (IRIS Center, 2010).

Darling-Hammond and colleagues (2017) identified seven key characteristics of effective PD, including PD that (1) "[is] content focused," (2) "incorporates active learning utilizing adult learning theory," (3) "supports collaboration, typically in job-embedded contexts," (4) "uses models and modeling of effective practice," (5) "provides coaching and expert support," (6) "offers opportunities for feedback and reflection," and (7) results in "sustained duration" (p. 4). Translated into our language, research-based PD includes training (i.e., explicit model, lead, and test format), coaching, and performance feedback to enhance implementation of key classroom practices across time (maintenance) and contexts (generalization). Each of these research-based systems elements (training, coaching, and performance feedback) may be organized to be supportive, culturally and contextually relevant, and sustained and sustainable.

ORGANIZING RESEARCH-BASED PD SYSTEMS TO SUPPORT TEACHERS

Now that we have discussed the principles that should guide our development of PD systems to support teachers, we turn to how to organize these supports. First, we provide an overview of PD support approaches, which briefly introduces how support will be provided (i.e., training, coaching, and performance feedback) and who may provide support. Then we ask you to link the content in this chapter with your growing knowledge of behavioral principles, and we illustrate how PD supports are linked to phases of implementation and the ABCs of behavior. Finally, we introduce an action-planning approach to help you develop, document, and organize the PD supports you will provide within your overall framework.

Overview of PD Support Approaches

How Will Support Be Provided?

Given our behavioral backgrounds, the PBIS community emphasizes function over form. In other words, rather than emphasizing "form" and thinking of a coach as a person with the title "coach" or thinking of performance feedback as necessarily being delivered by someone in a particular role (e.g., "coach"), we focus on the functions, or key activities and outcomes, of research-based PD supports (i.e., training, coaching, and performance feedback). For training, the key activities are based on explicit instruction (modeling, leading, and testing skill implementation). For coaching, the key activities include providing antecedent prompts and arranging (or rearranging) the environment to promote skill implementation. For performance feedback, the key activities include collecting data, evaluating data against a predetermined goal or criterion, providing feedback via graphic displays of data, problem-solving challenges, and celebrating successes in skill implementation. We describe these functions in much greater detail in Chapters 5 (training), 6 (coaching), and 7 (performance feedback).

Who Will Provide Supports?

In our experience, these research-based PD supports may be provided by a district coach or outside expert, a school coach or mentor, a peer, or oneself. Depending on the learning history of your teachers, available resources, and other contextual and cultural factors, you may elect to invest in systems that (1) rely on external supports (e.g., district-based coaches, outside experts); (2) invest in local supports (e.g., school-based coaches, mentors); (3) incorporate peer-based elements (e.g., professional learning communities, peer-based coaching); (4) emphasize self-management (e.g., self-monitoring, self-evaluating, and self-reinforcing one's own practice use); or (5) some combination of these approaches (e.g., district-based training, self-collected data, peer-based problem solving, and school-based celebrations of goals) to support your teachers. Table 4.1 illustrates a range of examples of how training, coaching, and performance feedback functions may be implemented by outside experts or district-based coaches, school-based coaches or mentors, peers, or oneself. As described, school leadership teams can select the combination of support approaches that fits their local context and culture, and each approach can be differentiated to meet the needs of all teachers (as you will learn in Chapter 8).

Behavioral Principles Applied to PD Systems to Support Teachers

In Chapter 1, we introduced the concept of the phases of learning, and in Chapter 2, we discussed the basic principles of behavior: types of antecedents (S^D, S^Δ, and S^{D-}), types of consequences (positive reinforcement, negative reinforcement, negative punishment, and positive punishment), approaches to teaching (establishing stimulus control, shaping, chaining, prompting). As we previewed in Chapters 1 and 2 and hinted throughout this chapter, these concepts directly map on to the way we've organized PD systems to support teachers.

TABLE 4.1. Overview of Support Approaches

	Training *Model, lead, test*	Coaching *Prompt, arrange environment*	Performance feedback *Data, evaluate, feedback*
Outside expert or district coach	• Provides explicit training (model, lead, test) on identified skill(s). • ***Assumes:*** Trainer is fluent in skills and has materials to facilitate explicit instruction.	• Expert or district coach provides antecedent prompts (via email, in person, or some combination). • Expert or district coach facilitates environmental changes to support teachers' implementation.	• Expert or district coach periodically observes teachers, collects data on trained skill(s), and creates graphs to monitor skill use across time. • Expert or district coach meets with each teacher to share data, problem-solve challenges, and celebrate successes.
School coach or mentor	• Provides explicit training (model, lead, test) on identified skill(s). • ***Assumes:*** Trainer is fluent in skills and has materials to facilitate explicit instruction.	• School coach or mentor provides antecedent prompts (via email, in person, or some combination). • School coach or mentor facilitates environmental changes to support teachers' implementation.	• School coach or mentor periodically observes teachers, collects data on trained skill(s), and creates graphs to monitor skill use across time. • School coach or mentor meets with each teacher to share data, problem-solve challenges, and celebrate successes.
Peer-based supports	• Accesses explicit training (model, lead, test) on identified skill(s). • ***Assumes:*** Online and print materials exist that provide explicit instruction.	• Peers develop a plan to collaboratively provide each other antecedent prompts (via email, in person, or some combination). • Peers facilitate environmental changes to support implementation.	• Peers periodically observe each other, collect data on trained skill(s), and create graphs to monitor skill use across time. • Peers meet to share data, problem-solve challenges, and celebrate successes.
Self-managed supports	• Accesses explicit training (model, lead, test) on identified skill(s). • ***Assumes:*** Online and print materials exist that provide explicit instruction.	• Each teacher develops a plan to provide antecedent prompts (via electronic prompting system, written notes, reminders, etc.). • Each teacher makes environmental changes to support his or her own implementation.	• Teachers self-monitor and collect data on trained skill(s), create graphs to monitor skill use across time. • Teacher self-evaluates skill use relative to a predetermined goal or criterion, recruits support (if needed) to problem-solve challenges, and celebrates (self-reinforces) successes.

Note. Each support described may be differentiated to meet individual teachers' needs.

First, we suggest that you consider the phases of learning when designing your approach to training, coaching, and performance feedback. Although there may be times that you want to focus only on skill acquisition or fluency, the most effective and efficient use of PD would program for maintenance and generalization of skill use from the beginning. Table 4.2 illustrates how the focus of training, coaching, and performance feedback may vary across phases of learning.

We also consider the ABCs when designing PD supports for teachers. For example, Figure 4.1 illustrates how coaching includes primarily antecedent functions (e.g., prompting, arranging the environment), how training focuses on developing behaviors, and how performance feedback is primarily a consequence-based strategy. In real life, these ABCs may function a bit differently for individual teachers. For example, a teacher who finds coaching supports aversive may be more reinforced by the fading of these supports (i.e., negative reinforcement) rather than the addition of celebrations (i.e., positive reinforcement) contingent on CWPBIS implementation. A different teacher may be reinforced by the attention provided during coaching supports, and he may request additional support even if data

TABLE 4.2. Emphasizing the Phases of Learning within Systems of Support

	Training	Coaching	Performance feedback
Acquisition	Training focuses on implementing the skill(s) accurately, prioritizing critical features, examples vs. non-examples to highlight accurate vs. inaccurate implementation, and practice.	Prompts focused on accuracy of skill implementation (e.g., prompting critical features).	Data collection and feedback focused on accuracy of skill implementation.
Fluency	Training provides opportunities to model, practice, and perform the skill at a desired rate.	Prompts initially focused on desired rate (or relevant dimension) of skill implementation.	Data collection and feedback focused on rate (or relevant dimension) of skill implementation.
Maintenance	Initial training includes sufficient practice to enable the skill to become automatic in the training context.	Prompts gradually faded to promote maintenance.	Data collection and feedback continue for previously trained skills to promote and monitor skill maintenance.
Generalization	Initial training programs for (1) the range of contexts in which the skill(s) should be implemented and (2) the range of ways in which the skills can be adapted to match the contexts.	Prompts focused on implementing the skill across a range of contexts and adapting implementation to fit the context.	Data collection and feedback occurs in novel situations and emphasizes appropriate adaptations of the trained skill(s) across contexts.

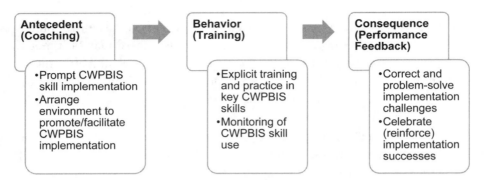

FIGURE 4.1. The ABCs of a PD system to support teachers.

do not indicate that further support is needed. Therefore, it's always important to consider the ABCs and function of an individual's behavior when designing and adjusting supports based on data, as behavioral principles operate at the individual level.

Road Map for PD Systems of Support for Teachers: Developing an Action Plan

At this point, you have learned the principles (i.e., supportive, contextually and culturally relevant, sustained and sustainable, and research-based) that should guide your decision making about PD supports; you have been introduced to research-based approaches to PD (i.e., explicit training, coaching, and performance feedback); and you can map these approaches back to the phases of learning and behavioral principles. Hopefully, you're feeling ready to take the next steps and learn the specific "what to do" details in subsequent chapters. Before you dive in, we give you a way to organize the remaining content that will become part of your framework or PD system for supporting teachers. For us, the most efficient and effective way to document our approach is an action plan. Think of an action plan as a glorified "to do" list—it will help you document key action steps, identify timelines, and assign tasks to members of your team. Another way to think of an action plan is as a road map for implementation . . . and now the chapter title makes sense!

As we described in previous chapters, we're assuming that most of you are reading this book because you are a member of a district or school leadership team or that you work in a role to support teachers either directly or via one of those teams. However, we also acknowledge that some of you may be individual teachers who are reading this book to get ideas for how to enhance your own practice, and we applaud your investment in your own professional growth. Action planning can occur at any of these levels (district team, school team, coach, or individual teacher), and documenting your ideas in an action plan is a key way to hold yourself (and team members) accountable for moving forward with systems-level implementation.

Figure 4.2 presents a sample CWPBIS systems-level action plan template. This template was designed to be used by a school- or district-level team, but it could be tweaked

Updated _____

Leadership Team Members

_____ (Behavior Coach)   _____ (Special Education)

_____ (Schoolwide PBIS Coach)   _____ (Specialist)

_____ (_____ Grade/Department)   _____ (Administrator)

_____ (_____ Grade/Department)   _____ (Add role)

Regular Meeting Times and Locations

Day: _____

Time: _____

Location: _____

Meeting Expectations

_____

_____

_____

_____

Behavioral Purpose Statement

_____

_____

_____

_____

Summary of Current Performance in Key Areas (Based on Data)

1. _____

2. _____

3. _____

Outcomes (Corresponding to Current Performance Areas)

1. _____

2. _____

3. _____

(continued)

FIGURE 4.2. Sample action plan template for a PD system to support educators.

Plan to Support Foundations (Priority, Resources, and Alignment):

Action	Who	When	Notes

Plan to Provide Explicit Training to Educators on Empirically Supported Classroom Practices:

Action	Who	When	Notes

Plan to Provide Educators with Coaching Supports (may be provided by coach, peer, or self):

Action	Who	When	Notes

(continued)

FIGURE 4.2. *(continued)*

Plan to Provide Educators with Performance Feedback (may be provided by coach, peer, or self):

Action	Who	When	Notes

Plan to Monitor Educators' Implementation of Classroom Practices:

Action	Who	When	Notes

Plan to Differentiate Supports Based on Data:

Action	Who	When	Notes

FIGURE 4.2. *(continued)*

to be used by an individual educator. This template prompts teams to (1) describe **team membership**, **routines**, and **norms**; (2) summarize current **data**; (3) identify contextually and culturally relevant **outcomes**; (4) ensure that the **foundational features** described in Chapter 3 (i.e., implementation phases and drivers) are addressed; (5) document plans for **research-based PD supports** (training, coaching, and performance feedback); (6) describe how teachers' implementation will be **monitored**; and (7) consider strategies to **differentiate supports** based on data. We recommend that you use this action plan as you progress through the remainder of the book.

SUMMARY

In this chapter, we (1) shared principles to guide your decisions about PD supports for educators, (2) provided an overview of research-based PD approaches, (3) mapped these PD approaches to phases of learning and behavioral principles, and (4) gave you a template for developing an action plan that will assist you with organizing knowledge and information presented in the remainder of the book. So, as you leave this chapter, it's time to get started on your action plan! You should already have the knowledge and information you need to complete the beginning sections (i.e., team, data, outcomes, and foundations). In Chapter 5, you learn about how to provide explicit training to educators. Chapter 6 helps you refine your ideas about how to provide coaching supports. Chapters 7 and 8 show you how to collect data to monitor teachers' implementation, refine your understanding of ways to provide performance feedback to teachers, and prepare to differentiate supports based on data.

PHASES OF LEARNING ACTIVITIES: CHAPTER 4

Acquisition

1. On a sheet of paper or in an electronic document, make yourself a glossary of the key terms and their definitions from the beginning of this chapter (similar to the one you made after reading Chapter 2). This document will come in handy as you read through the rest of the book.

2. Identify and define the four guiding principles of system selection, implementation, evaluation, and adaptation.

Fluency

1. Review the section on the importance of ensuring that supports are contextually and culturally relevant. Then identify the specific context and cultural considerations at your school that will impact your support of teachers' implementation of evidence-based practices. What will you and/or your team need to consider?

2. Review the action plan in Figure 4.2 and sketch out some preliminary ideas for an action plan at your school or in your classroom.

Maintenance

1. Review your school's or district's website. What language or information do you find that relates to supporting teachers' implementation of research-based practices? How does what you find align with what you've learned in this chapter (and others)? If you can't find any language related to implementation supports, what would you add to make the public aware of your team's efforts?

2. Review Figure 4.1 and re-create it, replacing the bullet points with specific implementation examples (e.g., what CWPBIS skills would you select for implementation and subsequent prompting? What would those prompts look like? How would you monitor the skill's use?).

Generalization

1. We mention that implementation supports must be sustained and sustainable. Develop a list of resources available at your school or district for supporting implementation. Identify any concerns you have about limited resources, and brainstorm realistic ways to implement sustained and sustainable supports given any constraints that you and your team face.

2. Locate any historical data you can find on past implementation efforts in your school or district related to curricular, social/behavioral, or other initiatives. Review those efforts in the context of what we've discussed in this chapter. Were those initiatives implemented according to the guiding principles we've mentioned? If so, what did that look like? If not, what should the implementers have considered prior to beginning their efforts?

CHAPTER 5

Designing Effective Training Activities for Classwide PBIS

CHAPTER OBJECTIVES

By the end of this chapter, you should be able to . . .

1. Describe the critical features of effective training.
2. Develop a plan for CWPBIS training, based on your local context, that includes the critical features.
3. Evaluate the effectiveness of your training activities.

Imagine This: You are a second-year administrator in your district, and you've been asked to work with the PBIS team to design the CWPBIS PD activities for the year. You are well aware, from past experiences and from reading the previous chapter of this book, that training alone won't be sufficient to drive changes in practices in your district, but you know that training is a critical part of an effective PD package. The PD release time for teachers in your district is limited, and you want to be sure you make the most of the time you have. You are also aware that, although most of your district's teachers have had insufficient (if any) training in CWPBIS strategies, some are quite skilled in their implementation of CWPBIS. You wonder about the best way to design effective training that meets the diverse needs of the staff. You turn to this chapter and sit down with your PBIS team to learn about designing and evaluating effective CWPBIS training activities for your district.

CRITICAL FEATURES OF EFFECTIVE TRAINING

As you likely remember from Chapter 4, training is one part of effective PD. Any training efforts should be paired with coaching supports (which we discuss in Chapter 6) and performance feedback (discussed in Chapter 7). In this chapter, we focus on what critical features of effective training look like and why they work. Then we examine how these critical features can be applied across different training environments. Finally, we discuss options for evaluating training outcomes and using evaluation data to inform future training opportunities.

In the previous chapter, we reviewed Darling-Hammond and colleagues' (2017) seven characteristics of effective PD. Four of those characteristics (i.e., content-focused, actively engaging, supporting collaboration, and modeling of effective practices) are specifically related to the training components of PD; the others related to coaching and PD reappear in subsequent chapters. Darling-Hammond and her colleagues found (and we agree!) that effective PD for CWPBIS practices includes explicit instruction in one or more specific skills and modeling effective practices (in addition to coaching and performance feedback). In this chapter, we explore each of these components of effective training and provide you with tools to develop a plan to implement and evaluate your training efficiently and effectively.

Explicit Instruction

Explicit instruction, similar to direct instruction (a research-based teaching approach employed frequently in K–12 education), is an approach to teaching new skills that generally progresses from teacher- (or trainer-) directed instruction and modeling (i.e., **model**) to guided practice (i.e., **lead**) to independent practice (i.e., **test**). Like direct instruction, the explicit instruction approach is research based and is appropriate for use across content areas and ages (Archer & Hughes, 2011; Brophy & Good, 1986). Below, we describe each of the components of explicit instruction (i.e., model, lead, test) in detail and provide examples.

Model

The model (or "trainer-led") phase of explicit instruction begins with the trainer first clearly identifying **learning objectives**; second, providing a clear **rationale** for the importance of implementing the specific practice(s) selected for training; and third, **operationally defining** the practice(s) being taught. The trainer then develops a series of direct demonstrations (i.e., models) of the practice to highlight the **critical features** and ensure that participants can identify what the practice(s) should look like in a classroom similar to theirs.

The first step when developing training on CWPBIS practices is clearly identifying and stating **learning objectives**. As educators, we are familiar with the process of developing academic and social skill lesson objectives for our students—it's what we do every day! Beginning with a clearly articulated learning objective helps us focus the content, examples, and activities in the lesson. The same process applies when designing the training piece of a PD package. Clearly articulating what learners (i.e., teachers and staff, in our case) will be able to do following training is a critical first step that shapes all training content and activities. Learning objectives should be written in observable and measurable terms and should identify a specific criterion for success. For example, "After this training, participants will be able to increase their use of specific praise statements and achieve the initial goal rate of one specific praise statement per minute during teacher-led instruction across three 15-minute observations." The instructional objectives selected will vary (i.e., they will be contextually appropriate) depending on the specific needs of your school and staff and should be guided by data. We discuss the process of using data to differentiate your PD in Chapter 8.

Once you have clearly identified one or more learning objectives for your training, the next step is **articulating the purpose and rationale** for learning this particular skill or CWPBIS practice. Each of the CWPBIS practices described in Chapter 1 is supported by research and has demonstrated a functional relation to specific improved outcomes for students and teachers. Explicitly identifying **why** a skill or CWPBIS practice is important (e.g., specific praise is associated with a wide range of improved student behavior across settings, demographics, and age groups) and **how** that practice will benefit students (e.g., increased achievement, more time on task) and teachers (e.g., improved student behavior, increased self-efficacy related to classroom management) gives teachers a reason to invest in starting to use or increasing their use of this practice in their classrooms.

Once you have articulated the purpose and rationale for training a particular skill (and hopefully have gotten some buy-in from your audience), you need to clearly **define the critical features** of the CWPBIS practice(s) you are training. Teachers (like anyone being taught a new skill) need to know exactly what the "active ingredients" of the practice are. Any training should begin with a clear definition of the practice(s) teachers should be able to implement following the training. The critical features of each of the CWPBIS practices are described briefly in Chapter 1 and in more detail in Simonsen and Myers (2015).

Once your participants have a clear understanding of the learning objectives, the rationale, and the critical features of the practice(s) on which they're being trained, the next step is the **demonstration** (or modeling) of what the practice looks like. There are many ways to model practices. For example, you (or the trainer) can (1) demonstrate the practice and even role-play with some of the participants; (2) employ video models that you create (surprisingly easy if you have working fluency with an iPad or smartphone with a camera feature) or access as part of already-created training materials; or (3) ask participants who have previously mastered the content to role-play, as long as they are comfortable doing so. When choosing your approach to demonstration, consider using models similar to the environment in which your participants will be implementing the practice (e.g., elementary schools, high schools, special education classrooms, relevant subject areas, demographics). Demonstrating what practices will look like in an environment similar to that in which the practices will be implemented allows participants to better understand what the practice looks like (and doesn't look like) in their context.

During demonstrations, be sure to highlight the critical features of the practice. For example, if you show participants a video of a teacher delivering a specific praise statement, draw attention to the positive verbal statement that named the specific student behavior— for example, "In that video clip, the teacher told the student that the student was doing an excellent job working quietly with his feet on the floor. What is the specific behavior that the teacher is praising?" Participants should be able to identify the critical features of a practice across a range of examples. Exposing participants to a wide range of examples during demonstration increases the likelihood that they will be able to generalize their use of the practice across settings. You may also choose to model one or more non-examples, but be sure to make it very clear what is a non-example to ensure that participants don't create a misrule while learning. For example, you could demonstrate saying "Good job" and "Good job meeting your responsibility as notetaker during this group task" after the same student behavior and ask participants which is the example of the target practice (i.e., specific praise) you're training, what the differences are between the examples, and why the example of specific behavioral praise is likely to be more effective than the non-example. Presenting examples and non-examples (along with careful explanations of both and clear contrasts between both) helps participants understand how practices that may appear to be similar to your target practice are in fact different (e.g., how opportunities to respond and specific praise differ, or how sarcasm and specific praise differ).

Lead

Now that your participants can identify the practice and have had an opportunity to see examples (i.e., the acquisition phase of learning), you can follow with opportunities for the participants to practice their newly learned skills (i.e., build fluency) during the "lead" phase of training. You will want to carefully design your practice activities to set your participants up for success. Consider using a range of practice opportunities that gradually increase the level of your participants' independence. For example, you could begin by asking participants to identify examples or non-examples of the practice that you generate (which could be a continuation of what you did as part of the demonstration, if you included examples and non-examples in your model). The next practice activity may be asking participants to work together to generate examples of the practice they have seen. Finally, ask participants to generate examples of the practice that they could use in their own classroom contexts. You have moved from simple discrimination (i.e., example or non-example) to production (i.e., generating original examples), increasing your expectations for your participants as they build fluency with the content. An additional benefit of a structured approach to increasingly independent practice opportunities is that you (as the trainer) have multiple opportunities to provide frequent feedback and to correct any misconceptions or errors early on, before your participants have had time to practice incorrectly.

Test

The last step in explicit instruction is the "test" phase. During this phase, you will provide your participants with a chance to practice their newly acquired target skill(s) independently and receive feedback. Ideally, this "test" should mimic real-life implementation as much as possible within the training context. Consider asking participants to role-play classroom scenarios using one or more of the CWPBIS practices they've learned, or ask participants to write out a script for how they would use a practice in their classrooms. By providing independent practice that "looks like" (to the greatest extent possible) what participants will need to do in their classrooms, you can ensure that your audience leaves the training with a high likelihood of being able to independently perform the skill in their classrooms (i.e., they will be able to generalize what they've learned by applying the skill in a different setting). In addition, this independent practice during the "test" phase (much like the "lead" phase) gives you the opportunity to provide specific feedback and encouragement to your participants and identify any teachers who may need additional supports with implementation.

See Table 5.1 for additional specific examples of what might be included during the model, lead, and test phases of explicit training. Figure 5.1 includes an example of a training script for specific praise. Feel free to use this for your own specific praise training, or use it as a model to develop your own training module.

Additional Considerations

In addition to the specific elements of the model, lead, and test phases of explicit instruction we've just described, researchers have suggested several other critical features of effective training that should be considered across each of these phases. To be truly effective, training should be actively engaging, collaborative, job-embedded and content-focused, and differentiated based on learners' needs.

Active Engagement

Active engagement is a critical component of effective training (Darling-Hammond et al., 2017). In K–12 classrooms, actively engaging learners is associated with a wide range of improved behaviors and student outcomes (Simonsen et al., 2008); engaged learners reap more benefits from instruction. Actively engaging participants during training increases the likelihood that participants will have an improved learning experience and increases opportunities for the trainer to assess teachers' learning during the training and for the participants to practice the CWPBIS strategies they are learning. Just as high rates of varied OTRs can increase active engagement in a K–12 classroom, high rates of OTRs can have the same results with adults. Consider providing multiple OTRs that vary between individual responses, unison responses (i.e., everyone responding together), mixed (i.e., unison and individual together, e.g., the "whip around" strategy, in which learners write down a response to a question and then share with the group), and other partner or collaborative learning activities (e.g., turn and talk, role play, peer instruction, "jigsaw" group activities in which each member has a specific contribution to make) to keep your OTRs diverse and engaging. Also, remember that OTRs can require various response modes such as verbal (e.g., choral or individuals responding to a posed question), gestural (e.g., thumbs-up, hand-raise), written (e.g., individual white boards, response cards), or technological (e.g., online survey tools). OTRs should focus the learners' attention on the content and will vary as you progress through the model, lead, and test phases of explicit instruction. See Table 5.2 for specific examples of what actively engaging adult learners can look like during training across the phases of explicit instruction. In general, consider providing (1) high rates of OTRs when describing the rationale for and critical features of the CWPBIS practice, (2) structured and interactive practice activities that set participants up for success during the lead phase, and (3) independent practice opportunities with feedback during the test phase.

TABLE 5.1. Specific Examples of Activities during the Model, Lead, and Test Phases of Explicit Training

Explicit training for CWPBIS practices	Examples
Model	
Clearly identify learning objectives.	• Following a training on specific praise, 90% of teachers will be able to generate three to four specific praise statements that would be contextually appropriate for their classrooms. • Following a training on OTRs, 80% of teachers will be able to revise a lesson plan to include three to four different types of OTRs.
Explicitly describe the rationale for each objective.	• Increased teacher rates of specific praise are associated with improved student behavior and learning. • Providing a variety of OTRs is an effective strategy for increasing student engagement and decreasing problem behaviors.
Clearly describe the critical features of each skill.	• Specific praise is a positive verbal statement that describes a specific behavior. • An OTR is a teacher behavior that elicits an observable response from a student.
Provide a range of effective models.	• Use video examples of teachers delivering specific praise statements in classrooms with a similar grade level or content focus as your participants. • Ask one or more of your teachers who have successfully implemented this skill to role-play or demonstrate for the group what the practice looks like in their classrooms. • Provide examples that cover the range of grade levels or subject areas covered by your participants.
Lead	
Provide a range of increasingly independent practice opportunities.	• Ask participants to identify whether a statement is an example of specific praise, then ask participants to generate examples they have seen together. • Ask participants to identify and count the OTRs in a video example, then ask participants to work together to script OTRs they could add to a lesson or video example. Finally, ask teachers to modify a lesson plan for their classes to increase the number or type of OTRs they will use.
Test	
Provide independent practice activities that are similar to "real-life" implementation.	• Ask participants to script a specific praise statement they could use in their classrooms. • Ask teachers to modify a lesson plan for their classes to increase the number or type of OTRs they will use by scripting specific examples.

Review and wrap-up

The focus of today's CWPBIS Training is **specific praise**.

First, what is specific praise?
• Research indicates that specific praise is a positive statement, typically provided by the teacher, after a desired behavior occurs (that is, the praise is delivered contingently on the behavior) to inform students specifically of what they did well.

Why provide specific and contingent praise?
• Research has indicated that increasing the number of behavior-specific praise statements contingently on expected behavior is consistent with increases in students' on-task behavior, attention to task, compliance, and academic performance (e.g., Simonsen et al., 2008).

What are some examples and non-examples of specific praise?

Examples of Specific Praise	Non-Examples of Specific Praise
During educator-directed instruction, a student raises her hand. The educator says, **"Thank you for raising your hand."**	During educator-directed instruction, students are talking over the educator, who says (while rolling his eyes), **"Gee, thanks for listening."** (*This is sarcasm, not specific praise.*)
A student enters the class during educator-directed instruction; the student walks quietly to his seat. The teacher walks over to the student and whispers, **"Thanks for entering the room quietly. That was very respectful."**	A student enters the class during educator-directed instruction and quietly walks to her seat. The teacher gives her a thumbs up. (*This is general and nonverbal.*)
After a student responds correctly by explaining the concept of conservation of energy, the teacher says, **"Nice job including all major points in your answer."**	During a physics lesson, the teacher **asks a group of students to explain** the concept of conservation of energy. (*This is an OTR, not praise.*)

(continued)

FIGURE 5.1. Example of training script for specific praise.

What are the critical features of specific praise?

- Deliver immediately after behavior.
- Specifically state the desired behavior demonstrated.
- Pair praise with other rewards (e.g., delivery of tokens or points) used with the class.

How will you use specific praise in your classroom?

- Write three or more specific praise statements that you will use in your classroom during educator-directed instruction.

- _____

- _____

- _____

How will you increase the likelihood that you will deliver specific and contingent praise?

- Self-management (definition):
  - According to Skinner (1953), we manage our own behavior in the same manner as we manage anyone else's—through "the manipulation of variables of which behavior is a function" (p. 228).
  - Self-management is engaging in one response (i.e., the self-management behavior) that affects the probability of a subsequent behavior (i.e., the target or desired behavior). For example, keeping a "to-do" list (which is a self-management behavior) may increase the likelihood that you "do" the things on your list (i.e., the target behaviors).
- Self-management in this training:
- We will ask you to (1) arrange your environment to increase the likelihood that you use praise (i.e., set goals and give yourself reminders); (2) self-monitor (count) your use of specific praise during a 15-minute segment of instruction; (3) self-evaluate (i.e., graph your specific praise rates daily and decide whether you met your daily goal), and (4) self-reinforce (i.e., give yourself a privilege on days you meet your goal).
  - *Arrange your environment.* Today, we will set an initial **goal** for your specific praise rate. Your goal is the criterion you will use to determine whether you can self-reinforce. This goal can be adjusted weekly based on the previous weeks' average. In addition, we'll ask you to select a strategy to **prompt** or remind yourself to use specific praise.
  - *Self-monitor.* Press button to advance **counter** each time you give one (or more) students specific praise during the selected 15-minute segment of educator-directed instruction.
  - *Self-evaluate.* Record total praise statements in the provided Excel spreadsheet and view the updated **graph** to determine whether you met your performance goal. (We will show you how to use the Excel spreadsheet.)
  - *Self-reinforce.* Select a **privilege** that you'll allow yourself (e.g., a cup of coffee on the way home, an extra 15 minutes of TV) each day that you meet your goal. It needs to be something you like and will allow yourself ONLY on days when you meet your goal.
- To help, we will send you weekly reminders about specific praise and ask you to email your updated graph in the Excel file (or upload it to a Dropbox). In that email, we'll also ask you to let us know if you adjusted your goal based on your previous week's performance.
- We will use the following table to further develop your self-management plan.

(continued)

FIGURE 5.1. *(continued)*

Estimate your current praise rate:	_____ specific praise statements per minute
Initial praise rate goal:	_____ specific praise statements per minute
Plan for increasing praise: *Identify how you will (1) prompt/ remind yourself to use praise, (2) use other strategies (e.g., script praise statements into your lesson) to increase praise, and (3) prompt/ remind yourself to self-monitor.*	(1) (2) (3)
Self-delivered reinforcement: *Identify the reinforcer you will deliver daily when you meet your goal.*	
Procedure for self-delivered reinforcement: *Identify when you will (1) enter your praise data, (2) determine whether you met your goal, and (3) reinforce yourself (i.e., how you will deliver/access your reinforcer).*	(1) (2) (3)
Procedure for email coaching: *Identify when you will check email to receive additional prompts and submit your data each week.*	

To track your data daily, you'll enter it into a spreadsheet. We will provide you with an example and show you how it works in our presentation.

FIGURE 5.1. *(continued)*

88

TABLE 5.2. Examples of OTRs across Explicit Instruction Phases

	Model	Lead	Test
Active Engagement	• Turn and talk: Does the rationale for this CWPBIS practice match a need in your classroom? • Choral response: What are the critical features of specific praise?	• Gesture response: Give a thumbs-up if this is an example of an OTR. • Partner work: With a partner, generate a list of two to three examples of specific praise statements you have seen.	• Role-play: With your team, create a role play in which you demonstrate the use of specific praise for a situation in your classroom. • Written: Script two to three examples of OTRs you can use in your classroom.

Collaborative and Job-Embedded

Collaboration is a critical element of effective PD (National Commission on Teaching and America's Workforce, 2016). Training provided within a district or a school, as opposed to training some isolated teachers at an offsite training or conference, provides opportunities for teachers to learn alongside those colleagues with whom they work each day in the environment in which the skills taught during the training will be implemented. The opportunity to collaborate with one another during training allows teachers to create a learning community focused on improving implementation. When planning your training, consider building in opportunities for participants to work collaboratively to identify, practice, and provide feedback to each other with respect to the critical features of the CWPBIS strategy you are training. Many of the OTR strategies described in the previous section (e.g., turn and talk, role play) promote collaboration while increasing the likelihood of teachers' active engagement in the learning process. The collaborative work that begins during the initial explicit training session(s) should be continued and encouraged as participants progress through the coaching and performance feedback elements of your PD plan. We cover coaching and performance feedback in Chapters 6 and 7, respectively.

Content-Focused

There is evidence that training focused directly on the specific content taught by educators is more effective than training focused on more generic pedogogical skills (Darling-Hammond et al., 2017). Consider this factor as you develop your plan for training teachers in CWPBIS strategies, as CWPBIS strategies are neither discipline-specific nor typically embedded in discipline-specific curricula. Trainers must work with teachers to ensure that each CWPBIS strategy is not taught in isolation but rather clearly linked to classroom content and context. For example, rather than simply defining an OTR and providing general examples, trainers should gather enough information about the context and participants prior to training to be able to describe and demonstrate how OTRs can be used within the seventh-grade math teacher's algebra curriculum or the first-grade team's reading curriculum. Doing so promotes generalization, and, as we've mentioned before, generalization is the goal of all learning.

Additionally, demonstrating how each CWPBIS strategy relates to other CWPBIS strategies supports teachers' use of CWPBIS skills in the context of their own curricula. For example, increasing OTR rates (first CWPBIS strategy) provides additional opportunities for delivering specific praise (second CWPBIS strategy) when students engage appropriately in the lesson. Make this connection and use context-specific examples. For example, if you are teaching a science lesson on the water cycle, begin by asking students to write down one thing they know about the water cycle or water in general (OTR), then ask them to turn and talk (OTR) about what they wrote. If pairs are talking quietly and staying on task, acknowledge them (specific praise). Bring the group together to share their responses (OTR) and acknowledge students who raise their hands, mentioning the specific behavior each time (specific praise). Similarly, when teachers deliver a brief error correction (e.g., "Remember, Cooper, if you want to share, raise your hand") followed by an opportunity fix the error (e.g., "Would you like to try again?"), students are engaged in an OTR (in this example, Cooper's hand-raise), and teachers have the opportunity to deliver a specific praise statement when the student performs the skill correctly (e.g., "Excellent, Cooper! Raising your hand is the respectful way to show you have something to add. What would you like to say?"). Ensuring that your training includes opportunities to link CWPBIS strategies to teachers' existing curricula and demonstrating how CWPBIS strategies work together increase the likelihood that teachers will understand how their newly learned CWPBIS skills fit into their classroom context and subsequently experience successful implementation.

Differentiated

Finally, effective training (like effective teaching) is designed to meet teachers "where they are" with respect to their CWPBIS strategy implementation. Ideally, we provide teachers with training on a specific skill or skill set where there is a demonstrated need as soon as that demonstrated need arises. For this to work, training must be shaped through careful data collection and evaluation. In Chapters 7 and 8, we describe ways to collect data on the implementation of CWPBIS strategies in your school or district and how to use those data to differentiate your training. For now, we assume that most teachers in your building or district have not yet been provided with explicit training in CWPBIS strategies and will need training in all CWPBIS strategies (i.e., Tier 1, or universal-level training). However, you may want to consider strategies to differentiate some elements of training even when developing the initial comprehensive scope and sequence of CWPBIS training. For example, consider providing options for choice with respect to the order in which CWPBIS strategies are trained, as teachers may perceive an immediate need for certain strategies; these strategies should be the initial starting point. You can also consider opportunities for teachers to progress through guided practice activities at different rates or even offer more experienced (and effective) teachers leadership roles within the training by asking them to help demonstrate strategies or provide feedback to newer teachers. As we say often in K–12 education, not all learners will progress at the same rate; this also holds true for adult learners. We visit this concept again in Chapter 8.

OPTIONS FOR DELIVERING TRAINING

Now that we have described critical features of effective training, let's consider the range of options for delivering CWPBIS training. As we described in Chapter 4, training (as well as coaching and performance feedback) can be delivered by an outside expert, a district- or school-based mentor, or peers; training can even be self-delivered. In addition to considering who will deliver the training in your school, also consider who will be trained. Training can be delivered to districtwide groups, school-based groups, grade-level (or other small) groups, or individuals. The critical features of CWPBIS training will not change based on the trainer or trainees, but some of the logistics may. For example, if you are working one-on-one with a peer to learn about implementing specific praise, you'll need to ensure that you have access to explicit instruction and sufficient opportunities for practice and feedback, just as you would encounter in a training delivered by an outside expert or district coach. You may look for webinars, instructional videos, or other available materials (e.g., training resources available at *www.pbis.org* or books such as this one and others in the Guilford Practical Interventions in the Schools series) for the "model" phase and create activities to build fluency for the "lead" and "test" phases. Similarly, if you are working with a small group of teachers (e.g., a grade-level team) to increase their rates of OTRs, you want to ensure that your training includes each of the critical features described in this chapter and provide grade-appropriate examples and non-examples, actively engage the team (perhaps they could role-play with one another), and potentially have them assess each other's implementation (i.e., the "test" phase). In Chapters 7 and 8, we discuss how and why you may select one delivery method over another to best fit the culture and context of your school and how to use data to deliver differentiated and targeted supports to groups or individuals within your school or district.

EVALUATING TRAINING OUTCOMES

As you have learned, whenever educators provide any kind of targeted instruction to learners, they must evaluate the effectiveness of that instruction. Training teachers in CWPBIS implementation is no different. After every training you conduct, you should have an efficient and effective way to collect data on both the participants' perceptions of the training and their progress toward the learning outcomes you identified when the training began.

Evaluating Perceptions

Although perception data won't tell you whether your participants are actually able to implement CWPBIS strategies in their classrooms, those data will provide useful information about which parts of the training participants felt were most helpful. A wide variety of questions can be included when evaluating teachers' perceptions of training. We recommend beginning with the following:

- Do participants feel that the training was effective?
- Do participants understand what CWPBIS is, and do they have a plan for implementation?
- Do participants know how to find additional support or resources?
- Do participants feel that the training was sufficiently engaging?

Participants' answers to these questions will help you make decisions about how you organize and use time in future trainings. The sample training evaluation form in Figure 5.2 provides an example of a way to collect this information. Using readily available electronic survey tools (e.g., SurveyMonkey, Google Forms) can make data collection an efficient process and allow you to aggregate those data quickly across participants.

Evaluating Outcomes

Although information about what participants liked and found useful (and maybe not so useful) about CWPBIS training is important and should be used to shape future trainings, we must also discern what participants actually learned during the training and can implement afterward. First, return to the learning objectives you identified at the start of your training. Each of those learning objectives should have been stated in clear, observable, and measurable terms with a specific criterion for success (e.g., "After this training, participants will provide students with an average of one observable opportunity to respond per minute and will be able to collect data on their rate of OTRs by using a golf clicker to track frequency of OTRs and dividing frequency by the number of minutes during which data were collected to determine the rate of OTRs."). Evaluating the outcomes of your training can be done by simply determining whether your learners met the learning objectives. The clearer and more specific your learning objectives are, the easier it is to determine whether they were met.

When evaluating our CWPBIS training, we should consider what the participants are able to do within the training context and (perhaps more important) what participants are able to do when they return to their classrooms. In other words, can participants use CWPBIS strategies independently during training (i.e., demonstrating fluency with those strategies), and can they implement them effectively in their classrooms (i.e., demonstrating generalization of those strategies)? In the training context, we can typically assess only the first of those two questions; we need additional coaching and performance feedback strategies (covered in Chapters 6 and 7, respectively) to assess actual implementation in the classrooms. Good news, though! Assessing participants' learning in the training context is relatively easy when using an explicit instruction framework. The "test" phase of instruction asks learners to demonstrate or perform a task independently. The key for you (as the trainer) is simply to document the extent to which your participants are successful with this task. For example, if you ask participants to script specific praise statements independently, what percentage of them correctly do so? Similarly, if you ask participants to role-play a scenario in which they deliver OTRs, what percentage of your participants deliver a high rate of varied OTRs? The answers to these questions help you assess the impact of your training

	Strongly Disagree	Disagree	Neither Agree nor Disagree	Agree	Strongly Agree
1. The CWPBIS training **balanced** big ideas with practical, relevant examples and applications.	1	2	3	4	5
2. The CWPBIS training used an **effective combination** of instruction and activities/teamwork time.	1	2	3	4	5
3. I can easily locate and access training materials and other CWPBIS **resources**.	1	2	3	4	5
4. As a result of attending this training, I have a detailed and doable **action plan** to guide implementation.	1	2	3	4	5
5. I have a detailed plan to collect and use **data** to guide implementation of CWPBIS strategies.	1	2	3	4	5
6. The training content kept me **engaged** and moved at a sufficient pace.	1	2	3	4	5
7. The trainers were **prepared** and knowledgeable.	1	2	3	4	5
8. The trainers were **organized** and followed an agenda.	1	2	3	4	5
9. The trainers were **effective** instructors.	1	2	3	4	5
10. The trainers were **respectful** of my views and opinions.	1	2	3	4	5

The most helpful/beneficial thing about training was . . .

One thing I would like to change/improve for the next training would be . . .

FIGURE 5.2. Sample CWPBIS training evaluation. Adapted with permission from *www.nepbis.org*.

on teachers' ability to use CWPBIS strategies successfully. With a well-planned and well-executed training, we expect that most (i.e., around 80%) of participants should be able to successfully meet your learning objectives. Some participants will likely need additional supports, which we discuss further in Chapter 8.

Evaluating Changes in Student Behavior

Ultimately, the purpose of any training for educators is to effect positive change for students, whether the intended results are improved academic achievement, improved social behaviors, or both. Although "proving" a connection between training and improved student outcomes would be impossible without large-scale, randomized control group research studies, we can certainly look for correlations between the implementation of a training and subsequent changes in student behavior and performance. For example, if we conduct a schoolwide training on reading interventions and the following year students make significantly higher gains in reading than they've ever done previously (without other specific instructional trainings or modifications), we could reasonably assume that our training had an effect on reading performance. Similarly, if we conduct CWPBIS training in a school and experience a 30% reduction in ODRs the following year (when rates had been stable), we could reasonably assume that the CWPBIS training had an impact on students' appropriate behavior. Without evaluating student outcomes, we cannot say that our training was effective. Even if we find that all participants enjoyed the training and are implementing every aspect of the content with fidelity, if there are no subsequent improvements for students, we have not met our goal. Be sure to take baseline (i.e., pretraining) data on any student variables of interest (e.g., behavior measures, academic measures) to compare with posttraining data.

SUMMARY

Effective training is one part of a larger PD package. We know that many teachers may not have had adequate preparation in managing classroom behaviors successfully, so providing high-quality, effective training is a critical first step in the effort to improve teachers' implementation of CWPBIS strategies. Effective training (1) uses an explicit instruction (i.e., model, lead, test) format, (2) actively engages participants in their learning, (3) is collaborative and job-embedded, (4) links to specific content or classroom contexts, and (5) is differentiated based on learners' needs. In this chapter, we described and provided examples of each of these components, discussed options for delivering training (i.e., who delivers and to whom), and introduced some considerations for evaluating training efforts. Explicit training is just the first step, though. In the next chapter, we discuss additional antecedent strategies to support teachers' implementation of CWPBIS practices—coaching and mentoring.

Acquisition

1. Use the CWPBIS training self-assessment provided in Figure 5.2 to evaluate a CWPBIS training you attend (or have attended in the past). Did the trainer implement all the critical features of effective CWPBIS training? What recommendations can you make?

2. Develop (or, if applicable, review and modify existing) training materials for one or more CWPBIS strategies. Be sure to include all the critical features of effective training.

Fluency

1. With another trainer, practice or role-play delivering CWPBIS training. Use the sample CWPBIS training planning tool in Figure 5.3 as an example. Provide each other with feedback on each of the critical features of effective training. Discuss observations from being both the trainer and the trainee. What worked? What didn't?

2. Practice delivering one phase (i.e., model, lead, or test) of CWPBIS training. Ask a peer to provide feedback on your use of active engagement, collaboration, and content-focused strategies (or record yourself and self-evaluate).

Maintenance

1. Select a CWPBIS strategy you have not trained before and develop materials to train that strategy effectively. Be specific about how you will address each phase of training (i.e., model, lead, test).

2. Consider your school or district context and develop a scope and sequence training plan that provides effective training on all CWPBIS strategies to all teachers and staff. Include evaluation measures and specific examples of contextual relevance.

Generalization

1. Review the critical features of effective training presented in this chapter, then consider how you would adapt a CWPBIS training for participants working in different settings (e.g., preschool, self-contained program, high school, alternative school, or juvenile justice facility). Identify potential challenges that may arise in different contexts and how your training could be adapted to fit that context.

2. Using the content in this chapter, create a plan to embed CWPBIS strategy training within discipline- or curriculum-specific training. Be specific about how the academic and CWPBIS content align, and use examples that incorporate both.

Model		
1. The training clearly identified one or more learning objectives in observable and measurable terms.	☐ Yes	☐ No
2. The training explicitly described the rationale for each objective.	☐ Yes	☐ No
3. The training clearly described the critical features of each CWPBIS skill.	☐ Yes	☐ No
4. The training provided a range of effective models that are similar to the context in which my participants will be implementing CWPBIS.	☐ Yes	☐ No
Lead		
5. The training provided a range of increasingly independent practice opportunities.	☐ Yes	☐ No
Test		
6. The training provided at least one independent practice activity that is similar to "real-life" implementation.	☐ Yes	☐ No
Additional Considerations		
7. The training included a high rate of varied OTRs to actively engage participants throughout the training.	☐ Yes	☐ No
8. The training maximized opportunities for collaboration utilizing naturally occurring connections between participants.	☐ Yes	☐ No
9. The training explicitly linked CWPBIS strategies to existing curriculum and content materials.	☐ Yes	☐ No
10. The training explicitly linked individual CWPBIS strategies to each other.	☐ Yes	☐ No
11. The training provided opportunities for differentiated activities and support throughout the training.	☐ Yes	☐ No
Evaluation		
12. Data were collected on participants' perceptions of the training effectiveness and will be used to guide future training.	☐ Yes	☐ No
13. Data were collected on the learning outcomes for all participants and will be used to guide future training.	☐ Yes	☐ No

FIGURE 5.3. Sample CWPBIS training planning tool.

CHAPTER 6

Coaching to Support Teachers' Implementation of Classwide PBIS

CHAPTER OBJECTIVES

By the end of this chapter, you should be able to . . .

1. Describe the antecedent features of effective coaching.
2. Develop a coaching action plan for CWPBIS implementation, based on your local context, that includes the critical features.
3. Evaluate the effectiveness of your coaching activities.

Imagine This: You've just completed a CWPBIS training for your district—congratulations! You feel great about how it went (after all, you followed the guidelines for explicit training in Chapter 5) and have data indicating that your teachers and staff can identify and describe each of the CWPBIS practices and were able to demonstrate those practices in the training context. However, you begin to worry about how much your teachers have to do on a daily basis, and you're concerned that they may forget to implement their newly learned CWPBIS practices or that they won't be able to successfully adapt those practices to their particular classroom context without additional support. You've heard that coaching is an important part of good PD, but you're not sure how to set up a system of coaching supports that fits within your existing resources and that will effectively support your teachers and staff. You bring a copy of this chapter to your next district leadership team meeting, and the team sets aside time to learn together about coaching: what it is and how it can be used to support CWPBIS implementation.

CRITICAL FEATURES OF EFFECTIVE COACHING

Coaching is an essential piece of a successful CWPBIS PD package and can increase the likelihood that CWPBIS strategies in which teachers are trained can be transferred into the classroom context effectively (Fixsen et al., 2005; Joyce & Showers, 2002; Lewis & Newcomer, 2002). As we discussed in Chapter 4, "coaching" can be defined as a set of functions that includes both antecedent and consequence strategies (Freeman, Sugai, et al., 2017). Look closely at our definition of "coaching," which differentiates the actions of coaching (i.e., specific behaviors) from a designated person (or "coach"). In other words, coaching is a set of functions or activities that can be delivered in a variety of ways by a variety of people. Coaching may even be delivered via technology or self-delivered, depending on context, need, and available resources.

In Chapter 4, we discussed how coaching should be solely focused on helping teachers improve their CWPBIS implementation, not focused on evaluating overall job performance and not connected to official evaluation procedures. Coaching is for support only; it is not intended to be an assessment mechanism. In most cases, the person or people doing the coaching should not be the person or people doing official performance evaluations. If these roles do need to overlap, each role should remain distinct, and the purposes of each meeting or activity should be clearly communicated. For example, saying "You indicate that you'd like to increase your rates of OTRs; let's talk about strategies that might work" is coaching. Saying "During my observation, I noted that your praise rates were very high and met expectations, but your rates of OTRs have fallen below the criterion we set for success" is evaluating.

Coaching behaviors can be separated into two separate (but related) categories. First, in this chapter, we discuss the antecedent functions of coaching; that is, which coaching behaviors increase the likelihood that teachers will implement CWPBIS practices as trained and with fidelity? In Chapter 7, we explore the consequence functions of coaching in our discussion of providing performance feedback to teachers; that is, which coaching behaviors increase the likelihood that teachers will *continue* to implement CWPBIS practices as trained and with fidelity? In the first part of this chapter, we focus on describing and providing examples of each of the functions (or actions) of coaching. Then we describe a variety of ways these functions can be delivered to individuals, to small groups, or at the school or district level. We close the chapter with a discussion of options for evaluating the effectiveness of your coaching supports. Let's get started!

Coaching Functions

The purpose of CWPBIS coaching is to set up teachers and staff members for implementation success. Coaching includes assessing current or prior knowledge and implementation, facilitating communication, promoting goal setting, prompting implementation, and providing content expertise to support the transfer of knowledge and skills learned in CWPBIS training into classroom practice.

Assess Knowledge and Implementation

Even before CWPBIS training officially starts, you can begin to set up teachers and staff members for success. Gather any information you can about your teachers' and staff members' prior knowledge and any current implementation strengths and weaknesses. This information will help you align CWPBIS training content and activities with your participants' specific implementation needs. You can gather and synthesize this information via self-assessment, surveys, walk-through observations, or a review of discipline referral patterns (see Chapter 7 for specific data collection options) prior to CWPBIS training. During training, you can continue to set up participants for implementation success by providing contextually specific and culturally relevant examples and practice opportunities to ensure that participants know what each CWPBIS strategy looks like and how each strategy can work in their specific classroom settings. If participants understand how CWPBIS training aligns with specific needs in their schools or classrooms, they are more likely to be actively engaged during training. Finally, assessing participants' knowledge and implementation after training provides data to shape and direct additional supports as needed and plan for next steps.

In addition, coaches should ensure that they have the requisite content knowledge to be able to provide adequate support to those whom they are coaching. Simply being "one chapter ahead" of participants is unlikely to lead to effective and sustainable training efforts. Coaches need to be fluent with content, able to apply the content across multiple settings, and able to communicate content in a clear and effective way, as we describe below.

Facilitate Communication

Facilitating clear, multidirectional communication is another critical coaching function. To do so, ensure that all teachers and staff have a clear understanding of the expectations for CWPBIS implementation (*prior* to preparing and training for implementation!), as well as an understanding of why CWPBIS implementation is a priority (i.e., How will CWPBIS benefit teachers, staff, and their students?). For example, if you are providing coaching, you could clarify that the specific CWPBIS strategy on which they focused during training (e.g., overt system of reinforcement) is expected to be implemented in all classrooms across the school. In addition, coaching should include clear communication to the teachers about the range of supports available and how to access those supports. For instance, a weekly newsletter or email reminder from those responsible for providing coaching supports could be a simple way to (1) remind teachers and staff members about a specific CWPBIS strategy on which to focus, (2) communicate the ongoing importance of implementing all CWPBIS strategies, and (3) remind recipients of available supports and how those supports can be accessed, if needed.

In addition, facilitating communication between and across teachers and staff in a school or district can promote collaboration and help teachers support each other more effectively. For example, online discussion boards or designated times to share implementation successes and challenges during grade-level team meetings could facilitate communication and collaborative supports. Finally, providing a communication link (and encouraging ongoing communication) between trainers and participants helps ensure that participants understand the purpose of CWPBIS training and that the training (and follow-up support) fits the specific context in which participants will be implementing CWPBIS strategies. Trainers can use schoolwide data both to determine which components of CWPBIS content should be emphasized during training and to gain insight into particular aspects of school climate and culture that may impact CWPBIS implementation. This iterative process will help trainers ensure that their content and delivery are aligned with the specific needs of participants and appropriate for the context in which CWPBIS will be implemented.

Promote Goal Setting

After establishing clear, multidirectional channels for communication, the next key function of coaching is to promote goal setting for training participants. Goal setting helps focus implementation efforts on one or two key strategies that align with a high-priority need in a particular classroom or context. For example, rather than working to improve her overall classroom management (which is neither observable nor measurable), a teacher may set a goal focused on improving her rates of OTRs during key instructional times or improving her frequency of prompting prior to transitions. Effective coaching helps teachers select and develop appropriate goals that align with their specific contextual needs. Goals should be challenging (but realistic), written in observable and measurable language that allows teachers to clearly identify what the objective (i.e., target behavior and desired intensity of implementation) looks like, and include a specific criterion so teachers will know when they have reached the goal (e.g., two OTRs per minute, or an average of 30 OTRs per 15 minutes of instruction). Setting goals for teachers related to suggested rates of skill use and a range of examples demonstrating effective implementation will help teachers identify goals that are likely to lead to improved outcomes for students.

Prompt Implementation

Prompting implementation is another critically important function of coaching. As you might remember from Chapter 2 (and if not, this definition should prompt your behavior of remembering!), prompting is adding a stimulus to the environment (i.e., a prompt) that increases the likelihood that a person engages in a behavior. After CWPBIS training, teachers may have the knowledge and skills they need to implement CWPBIS strategies; however, teachers always face competing district and school initiatives (not to mention bearing the responsibility for educating a room full of students who may be in dire need of CWPBIS) and may struggle to implement CWPBIS strategies in their own classrooms if they don't receive additional support. Prompting can help teachers remember to focus on implementing the CWPBIS strategies they have learned. For example, a PBIS coach (or other person responsible for coaching support) can send an email to remind staff to focus on a specific strategy identified as a schoolwide or team-level goal (e.g., "Remember, we're working on increasing our rates of specific praise by 50% this month!"), or teachers can prompt themselves by adding a sticky note to their lesson plan books to remind themselves to provide specific praise. Those responsible for providing coaching supports may also model CWPBIS strategies for teachers, if needed, or provide additional examples for teachers who are not sure how a specific strategy fits in their classroom context. We've provided examples of email prompts for specific praise in Figure 6.1.

Week 1	Hi, everyone:
	We hope you're having a great Monday! We enjoyed meeting with you last week.
	As promised, this is your first weekly email reminder about specific praise. Remember, "specific praise" is contingent (delivered immediately after the behavior), specific (names the desired behavior exhibited), and positive.
	"Nice hand raise!" and "Thank you for actively listening" are examples of brief specific praise statements.
	Keep on counting, graphing, reviewing your data, and reinforcing yourself when you meet your goal, and please let us know if you have any questions.
	Thank you!
Week 2	Hi, everyone:
	Happy Monday! We hope you had a great weekend.
	This is your weekly reminder about specific praise. Remember, effective praise is contingent, genuine, and specific. **Specific** means that you name the behavior when you provide the praise statement (e.g., "Thank you for quietly finding your seat").
	Keep on counting, graphing, reviewing your data, and reinforcing yourself when you meet your goal, and please let us know if you have any questions.
	Thank you!
Week 3	Hi, everyone:
	Happy Monday! We hope you had a nice weekend.
	This is another weekly reminder about specific praise. "Catch 'em being good!" Specific praise (i.e., praise that names the behavior) is associated with a variety of desired outcomes for students, including both increases in academic and prosocial behaviors and decreases in disruptive and off-task behaviors.
	Keep on counting, graphing, reviewing your data, and reinforcing yourself when you meet your goal, and please let us know if you have any questions.
	Thank you!
Week 4	Hi, everyone:
	Happy Monday! We hope you had a nice weekend.
	It's time for your weekly reminder about specific praise. Praise that specifically names the behavior is not only good for your students, but we've found that it helps us focus on the positives throughout the day, and we go home thinking more about the positive things that happened during the day rather than things that didn't go so well.
	Keep on counting, graphing, reviewing your data, and reinforcing yourself when you meet your goal, and please let us know if you have any questions.
	Thank you!

FIGURE 6.1. Example of emails to prompt for specific praise.

Provide Content Expertise

Finally, even if your training participants receive high-quality, explicit CWPBIS training that includes all critical components described in Chapter 5, they may require more detailed information or additional examples to help facilitate implementation across the range of classrooms in your school or district. Coaching provides a link to additional or outside resources (e.g., in-person assistance and additional training, if needed; access and direction to helpful resources) that can support the development of content expertise within your school or district, as appropriate. Understanding when and why to use each CWPBIS strategy and how to modify a strategy to better meet the needs of students in a particular context could require access to behavioral competence that may not yet exist in your building or district, which is why the coach must possess content expertise (as mentioned previously). Settings in which students are likely to have more intensive behavioral needs and require additional behavioral supports (e.g., special education classrooms, alternative schools) will require increased precision and more attention to contextual details during CWPBIS implementation and a more in-depth understanding of the behavioral theory (e.g., reinforcement, extinction, stimulus control) behind each of the CWPBIS strategies. Coaching supports can meet the need for additional content expertise by providing teachers with (1) access to (or a synopsis of) new research or resources that may help with implementation, (2) information about local workshops or courses on behavioral theory that may support CWPBIS implementation, or (3) more targeted consultation and problem-solving support for teachers as needed. Access to additional information and behavioral competence can increase the likelihood of successful CWPBIS implementation for all teachers, and coaching supports can facilitate acquisition to appropriate content and competence.

OPTIONS FOR DELIVERING COACHING

Now that we've described the key functions of coaching, let's focus on the "who" and the "how" of these coaching functions to best support teachers in your school or district. In Chapter 4, we mentioned that coaching functions can be provided by an internal or external coach, peers, or even self-delivered. Thinking about coaching as a set of functions rather than as a specific person (i.e., a coach) allows flexibility for schools and districts when developing a coaching system that fits within the context of the school and considers existing school and district resources. The goal is not to provide "a coach" for each teacher but, as we stated previously (in slightly different terms), to have a system in place so each teacher can receive (1) support to assess his or her CWPBIS implementation, (2) clear communication, (3) help with goal setting, (4) prompting, and (5) additional behavioral expertise, as needed. Table 6.1 provides examples of how different coaching functions might look across different coaching provider options (i.e., internal–external coach, peer, or self). District or school coordinators can use the examples in Table 6.1 to identify (or generate ideas for) options for delivering each coaching function that are most appropriate for their school(s), small groups, and individual teachers.

When developing a coaching support system, begin by establishing a universal (i.e., Tier 1) level of coaching that will meet the needs of most teachers and increase the likelihood of their implementing CWPBIS practices reliably and with fidelity. Then identify and develop options for intensifying coaching supports for teachers who need additional help. We discuss intensifying supports for teachers in Chapter 8; this chapter's focus is on providing a universal, accessible level of coaching support for all teachers, which will help the majority of teachers successfully transfer their learning from the training context into their

TABLE 6.1. Examples of Coaching Functions across Different Delivery Options

Coaching function	Internal/external coach	Peer	Self
Assess knowledge and implementation	• Conduct walk-through observations. • Conduct staffwide electronic survey of CWPBIS knowledge and current practices.	• Grade-level groups observe each other and discuss current strengths and weaknesses. • Use the first 5 minutes of each team meeting to review data related to CWPBIS implementation.	• Self-assess CWPBIS implementation to identify areas of need. • Video or audio record a lesson to review your current implementation.
Facilitate communication	• Graph current implementation strengths and weaknesses to guide training content and activities. • Use online survey tools and data dashboards to collect and disseminate information about CWPBIS implementation to everyone involved.	• Work in peer learning groups to identify common strengths and needs with respect to CWPBIS implementation. • Use online discussion board platforms to encourage teachers to communicate across grade-level or school groups.	• Request training or support for specific CWPBIS needs. • Share your implementation successes with others on social media, via a school newsletter, or other appropriate platform.
Promote goal setting	• Use schoolwide data to identify whole group implementation goals. • Mentors work with new teachers to identify specific CWPBIS goals.	• Grade-level teams develop implementation goals together. • Teachers select and join a professional learning community (PLC) focused on the CWPBIS strategy they want to improve.	• Self-assess and set a clear implementation goal. • Share your goal or goals with a mentor teacher or peer. • Identify a preferred reinforcer and reward yourself when you meet your goal.
Prompt implementation	• Send an email to remind all staff to focus on implementing the CWPBIS practice they identified in their goal. • Use bug-in-ear or other technology to prompt specific skill use for teachers needing more intensive support.	• Teamed teachers (or teachers and paraprofessionals) can provide visual prompts to each other to remind each other to deliver specific praise rates. • Grade-level teams can reserve meeting time for discussion and prompts for implementation in their grade-level meeting agenda.	• Set a silent alarm on a phone as a reminder to deliver specific praise (or other CWPBIS strategy). • Add notes to your lesson plan book or teacher guide about how you plan to increase OTRs.
Provide content expertise	• Provide consultation and support to adapt CWPBIS implementation to more intensive contexts. • Regularly share new research or relevant examples with teachers and internal coaches.	• Work in teams to record video examples of CWPBIS strategies in your school or district. • Pair teachers who are strong CWPBIS implementers with those needing additional support.	• Review the classroom resources provided on *www.pbis.org* to learn more about effective implementation. • Enroll in an online or local behavior course or attend a webinar related to CWPBIS.

classrooms. You can use the action planning for coaching tool in Figure 6.2 to start shaping and documenting your plan for developing a comprehensive system of coaching support.

EVALUATING COACHING OUTCOMES

Now that you have started planning how to provide coaching supports in your school and district, consider how you will evaluate and adjust your action plan after implementation. When we evaluate a school's SWPBIS framework, we examine data related to fidelity of implementation and student outcomes. We can evaluate coaching by looking at these same categories of data. First, evaluation of your coaching action plan should measure teachers' access to coaching, or the fidelity of implementation of your coaching plan. In addition, any evaluation plan should measure the outcomes of coaching, or the extent to which teachers are able to successfully implement CWPBIS strategies in their classrooms.

Access to Coaching

Before you can assess the effectiveness of the coaching support available in your school or building, you need to determine whether all teachers have access to that support. That is, to what extent is your coaching action plan being implemented as intended? How you collect this information will vary based on the specific way(s) coaching is being delivered in your building. One simple way to evaluate coaching access is through a **coaching log**. This log should be accessible to and completed by everyone involved in carrying out coaching functions, and it should match the specific needs of your school or district. At a minimum, your log should collect information related to when coaching takes place, the specific coaching function provided, who provided the coaching, and who was coached. Consider collecting brief notes or other anecdotal information about the specific coaching activity and any issues that arise. We provide an example of a coaching log in Figure 6.3. By regularly collecting and reviewing information collected via a coaching log or other means, a district or school leadership team can assess the extent to which their coaching plan is being implemented as intended. Teams should ask the following questions on a regular basis as they compare the coaching log to the overall coaching implementation plan:

1. Are all coaching functions being provided in our school or district?
2. Do all teachers have access to all coaching functions?
3. Do teachers who need additional support have access to additional coaching?

If the answer to any of these questions is "no," the team needs to develop additional action plan items to ensure that coaching supports are in place with fidelity across the school or district prior to evaluating the effectiveness of the coaching supports. If the answer to each of these questions is "yes," the team should assess outcomes associated with coaching (described briefly below and in detail in Chapters 7 and 8), celebrate successes (of course!), and continue to monitor implementation across time.

Coaching function	How will this be delivered?	Who is the target group?	How frequently will we do this?	What resources do we need?	How will we evaluate?
Assess prior knowledge and implementation					
Facilitate communication					
Promote goal setting					
Prompt implementation					
Provide content expertise					

FIGURE 6.2. Action planning guide for coaching.

Date	Coaching function provided	By whom?	Group coached	Coaching notes
9/14	Prompting	School behavior coach	Whole staff	Posted reminders of the schoolwide CWPBIS implementation goals in the teachers' lounge
10/13	Prompting	Grade-level team leaders	Whole staff	Grade-level leaders reminded all teachers to focus on increasing specific praise rates this month
11/15	Provide content expertise	School psychologist	Special education teachers	Provided additional information about using behavioral theory to guide and adjust implementation in more intensive settings

FIGURE 6.3. Example of a coaching log.

Outcomes of Coaching

Once you have determined that your coaching action plan is being implemented as intended (i.e., with fidelity), you can turn your attention to determining whether teachers are benefiting from the coaching activities you have put in place; that is, are they meeting the overall objectives of CWPBIS training with coaching supports in place? The primary purpose of coaching is to help teachers transfer knowledge acquired during CWPBIS training into specific behaviors in the classroom (i.e., generalization). Therefore, the primary measure of our coaching effectiveness should be CWPBIS implementation in each classroom in which coaching supports are available and in place. Chapter 7 provides an explanation and examples of how to measure CWPBIS implementation, including options for collecting those data efficiently.

SUMMARY

Coaching is an essential part of an effective PD package, providing a critical link between training in CWPBIS content and implementation of CWPBIS in the classroom. Coaching can be conceptualized as a set of functions rather than a job title or a group of behaviors performed by one person. In this chapter, we described the basic functions of coaching and provided examples of assessing knowledge and implementation, facilitating communication, promoting goal setting, prompting implementation, and providing content expertise. We also discussed and provided applied examples of how each of these functions could be delivered by an outside expert, by an internal coach or peers, or self-delivered. School and district leadership teams can use the examples provided in this chapter in conjunction with the action planning guide (i.e., Figure 6.2) to develop a comprehensive coaching plan that ensures that all teachers have access to each of these basic coaching functions. Finally, we closed the chapter with a discussion of how to evaluate your coaching plan by assessing access to coaching functions (i.e., fidelity of coaching support implementation), as well as the implementation outcomes associated with the coaching supports you have put in place. In Chapter 7, after a discussion of data collection, we explore performance feedback, the final element of effective PD (and the consequence function served by coaching). Soon, you will have all of the information you need to initiate a comprehensive and effective PD plan for your school and district, and we hope you will be able to generalize what you've learned within these pages to your professional practice.

PHASES OF LEARNING ACTIVITIES: CHAPTER 6

Acquisition

1. Create a contextually appropriate coaching log (or modify an existing one) for your school or district based on the example we shared in Figure 6.3. What would you need to change, and why?

2. Review the coaching process in a school within your district. Use the tools in this chapter to determine whether all the coaching functions are represented and whether all teachers have access to effective coaching. Consider creating a checklist to help with your review.

Fluency

1. With another coach (or person responsible for providing coaching supports), select one or more coaching functions discussed in this chapter. Review options for delivering that element of coaching and develop materials you could use in your school (e.g., draft emails for prompting, templates for goal setting).

2. Practice delivering one of the critical features of coaching discussed in this chapter to a small group in your school. Ask a peer to provide feedback on your delivery of the critical feature and develop a plan for improvement based on the feedback you receive.

Maintenance

1. Select a coaching function you have not provided before (or one with which you routinely struggle) and develop materials or procedures for providing that support to teachers in your school or district.

2. Develop a coaching action plan that fits the needs and resources available in your school or district. What are some of the specific contextual factors that you'll need to consider while developing your plan?

Generalization

1. Review the critical features of effective coaching presented in this chapter, then consider how you would adapt your coaching plan for participants working in different settings (e.g., pre-school, self-contained program, high school, alternative school, or juvenile justice facility).

What, contextually, would need to change? Identify how you would collect the information you'd need to develop a contextually appropriate plan for that setting.

2. Using the content in this chapter, create a plan to embed CWPBIS coaching within a discipline- or curriculum-specific coaching plan. How could supporting teachers' implementation of CWPBIS practices align with those supports intended to improve teachers' instructional or content delivery? Make specific connections.

PART III

Data-Based Decision Making to Support Teachers' Classwide PBIS Implementation

CHAPTER 7

Data Collection Systems and Performance Feedback

CHAPTER OBJECTIVES

By the end of this chapter, you should be able to . . .

1. Describe efficient and effective tools for collecting data on teachers' use of CWPBIS strategies and student outcomes.
2. Select a tool (or tools) that best matches your needs and available resources.
3. Use the data to guide supports and provide performance feedback to teachers.

Imagine This: You have just delivered an explicit, comprehensive, and very effective (if you do say so yourself!) training on a specific CWPBIS practice, and you've sent out reminder emails to teachers to encourage them to use the practice. Now, you're asking yourself, did your training and prompting approach work? You know that you'll need to collect data to determine whether you're meeting your CWPBIS implementation goals, so you have to think about some efficient and effective data collection methods. Finally, once you've determined the type of data you want to collect and how you'll collect those data, you'll be ready to move to the third component of effective PD: performance feedback.

Supporting teachers' implementation of CWPBIS practices efficiently and effectively can be challenging for many administrators, coaches, and others in positions to provide PD and offer help. In order to determine the best way to provide support, supporters must collect and monitor data on teachers' implementation of CWPBIS practices to (1) evaluate the effectiveness of the support they've provided, (2) provide performance feedback on teachers' practices (a component of effective PD), and (3) guide further supports for educators. Data collection and monitoring processes may pose some challenges for those supporting

111

teachers' CWPBIS implementation. We hope that this chapter will help you select efficient and effective data collection processes that will facilitate supporting implementation of CWPBIS practices and plan your delivery of performance feedback. Although there are multiple ways to assess and monitor teachers' instructional practices, in this chapter, we have selected tools that align most closely with the empirically supported practices within CWPBIS.

We begin this chapter by describing tools and resources designed for observers (e.g., administrators, coaches, peers) to use when monitoring teachers' overall use of CWPBIS. Then we provide an overview of self-assessment tools teachers can use to assess their own practices and discuss ways to collect data on discrete skills. Remember, the goal is to collect data that will be useful in decision making: It's about quality, not quantity. Collecting too many types of data too frequently could drain your school or district resources and may lead to teachers' feeling overly scrutinized. After we've reviewed a range of options for data collection, we present guidelines for selecting an appropriate tool or tools based on the needs and resources available in your school. Finally, we describe how to use data to provide performance feedback to support teachers' ongoing growth.

OPTIONS FOR EFFICIENT AND EFFECTIVE DATA COLLECTION

Observer Checklists

When you think about collecting data on teachers' use of CWPBIS practices, you probably think first about conducting a classroom observation. Classroom observations are a tried-and-true way to gather accurate information on teachers' use of CWPBIS practices. Below, we recommend several observation tools that are closely aligned with CWPBIS practices. The measure you select depends on the resources you have available for collecting data and the level of detail you need to guide your decision-making process. Many of these tools may be completed by a variety of trained observers (e.g., behavior coach, mentor, peer, administrator).

Classroom Management Observation Tool

The Classroom Management Observation Tool (CMOT; Simonsen et al., 2020) was developed to align directly with CWPBIS practices. The CMOT is designed to be used by any observer (e.g., principal, behavior coach, peer) who has some experience as a classroom teacher and a basic understanding of CWPBIS practices. The CMOT is completed after a 15- to 20-minute observation of a teacher's instruction. The measure itself consists of six yes-or-no items related to classroom structure and expectations (critical components of effective classroom management, as indicated by research) and four items on positive and proactive classroom practices that are rated on a four-point scale. Scores on each item can be used to identify schoolwide priorities for PD and may be used to monitor performance across time, but we need more research to support this use of the CMOT. While the CMOT is still under development, we are hoping it will be among the most efficient tools available (and it's free!).

Classroom Strategies Scale

The Classroom Strategies Scale (CSS; Reddy, Dudek, Fabiano, & Peters, 2015; Reddy, Fabiano, Dudek, & Hsu, 2013) provides the observer with information about instructional strategies and behavioral management practices, including all of the CWPBIS practices. Specifically, the CSS measure includes counts of six discrete skills, 26 items related to instructional strategies, and 23 items related to behavior management. The CSS is designed to be completed after two or more 30-minute observations within 7 days. The CSS also has a complementary teacher report form that includes 26 items on instructional management and 23 items on behavior management.

Classroom Assessment and Scoring System

The Classroom Assessment and Scoring System (CLASS; Pianta, La Paro, & Hamre, 2008) is a comprehensive observation system that measures student and teacher behaviors in three areas: emotional support, classroom organization, and instructional supports. Observers receive 2 days of formal training prior to using the CLASS. The developers suggest that a 2-hour observation yields the most accurate and reliable picture of the teacher–student interactions in a classroom. The CLASS has been validated across pre-K–12 grade settings; however, it does not directly align with the CWPBIS practices.

Self-Assessment Checklists

Although observer checklists such as those listed above can be an effective way to collect data, they are not the only means of gathering information related to CWPBIS practice implementation. Sometimes, finding qualified observers (or any observers!) can be a challenge. Often, teacher self-assessments can be a more efficient way to gather information. Unfortunately, given the constant demands on a teacher's attention, teachers may lack the time or knowledge to accurately self-assess their CWPBIS practice implementation. Those providing PD in CWPBIS can make teachers' self-assessment easier and more accurate by ensuring that teachers have a clear picture of what the target CWPBIS practice(s) look like (e.g., by offering an overview of CWPBIS practices in a faculty meeting) and by setting aside a specific time for teachers to complete the self-assessment (e.g., at a faculty or team meeting after a target lesson or instructional time). In some cases, it may be helpful for teachers to record a specific lesson (e.g., by using the voice recorder or camera feature on a smartphone or tablet) and then complete a self-assessment after watching or listening to the recording.

A variety of teacher self-assessments of classroom management practices are available, several of which we discuss below. The specific self-assessment measure selected should depend on teachers' prior knowledge of CWPBIS practices and the specific practices you are most interested in assessing. In our discussion of observer checklists, we focused on measures that most closely aligned with CWPBIS practices; we do the same for our discussion of self-assessment measures. Please note that the self-assessment measures we describe below do not (at the time of this book's publication, at least) have established psychometric properties (i.e., reliability and validity) and should not be used for high-stakes decision making. Although we hope that teachers will assess their implementation skills accurately and honestly, we sometimes make errors when self-reporting, both unintentional and intentional. (After all, have you ever embellished your own self-assessment, perhaps when asked by your doctor about your exercise regimen, or overestimated your own skills when agreeing to perform a task, such as karaoke?)

Classroom Management: Self-Assessment Revised

The Classroom Management: Self-Assessment Revised (CM:SAR; Simonsen, Fairbanks, Briesch, & Sugai, 2006) was developed specifically to assist teachers with evaluating their implementation of CWPBIS practices in their classrooms. The CM:SAR provides guidance on counting specific CWPBIS practices (e.g., positive and negative student contacts, OTRs) and then asks teachers to rate themselves in each of the five critical CWPBIS areas. Teachers read a brief statement and circle "yes" or "no" based on their self-reflection. "Yes" ratings can be tallied to yield an overall classroom management score. (You'll notice that this tool may also be used by observers. The CM:SAR was an early classroom management self-assessment checklist that, over the years, evolved into the CMOT mentioned above.)

Missouri SW-PBS Teacher Self-Assessment of the Effective Classroom Practices

Teachers using the Missouri SW-PBS Teacher Self-Assessment of the Effective Classroom Practices (Missouri Schoolwide Positive Behavior Support, 2018) are asked to self-assess their implementation of eight effective classroom strategies, all of which align with CWPBIS practices. Teachers are asked to consider each of the eight effective practices and check a box if they have completed three or four specific tasks related to each area.

Classroom Practices Self-Assessment

The Classroom Practices Self-Assessment (Borgmeier, Loman, & Hara, 2016) is a 25-item scale with 19 items focused on classroom management and six focused on instructional practices. Teachers rate each item as "in place" (two points), "partially in place" (one point), or "not in place" (zero points). This Classroom Practices Self-Assessment measure covers all of the CWPBIS practices and provides a way to calculate an aggregate overall score based on the responses to each item.

Measuring Discrete Practices

The observer and self-assessment checklists discussed above can provide useful information on teachers' overall implementation of CWPBIS practices. At times, though, you may prefer to collect information on the rate or use of a specific CWPBIS skill. If so, you'll want to consider ways to measure discrete CWPBIS skills or practices. Teachers and observers (e.g., principal, coach, peer) can use the data collection options described below to assess and monitor implementation of teachers' use of CWPBIS practices and to provide feedback to teachers to improve their implementation of CWPBIS. (If some of these data collection options sound familiar to you, it's likely because we often recommend some of these same options for collecting data on students' behavior; e.g., Simonsen & Myers, 2015).

Event Recording

For discrete practices that are similar in duration and occur at a rate low enough to count easily (e.g., specific praise statements, OTRs, specific error corrections), counting or tallying may be the simplest and most effective way to collect data on teachers' implementation of those practices. Teachers or observers can simply count each time they observe the target skill(s) during an observation. The tally (i.e., number of events) can be recorded by making a mark on a piece of paper, using a golf counter or other "clicking" device, or with an app designed for data collection. This total number can then be divided by the total number of minutes observed to obtain a rate (i.e., occurrences per minute) for the observed skill. For example, a teacher could use a golf counter to record each time he or she provided a student with specific praise during a 30-minute lesson. At the end of the lesson, the teacher would divide the total number of recorded praise statements by the total number of minutes (i.e., 30) of the lesson to calculate the average rate of praise statements per minute.

Duration or Latency Recording

Timing (i.e., recording when a behavior starts and when it stops) is the simplest way to record information if you are interested in the duration (i.e., total time) of a practice (e.g., active supervision) or the latency (i.e., time elapsed) between a student behavior and teacher response (e.g., time between a student following the expectations and the teacher providing specific praise). Duration data can be collected by using a watch, a stopwatch, or the timer on a smartphone: Look at the watch or start the stopwatch or timer when the teacher begins to engage in the practice and look at the watch or stop the stopwatch or timer when the teacher stops engaging in the practice, then record the amount of time. To collect latency data, look at your watch or start the stopwatch or timer when the student behavior occurs and look at your watch or stop the stopwatch or timer when the teacher behavior occurs. Duration and latency data collection procedures work best when the practice you are observing has a clear beginning and end and when you are interested in how long a behavior lasts (i.e., duration) or the time elapsed between an antecedent stimulus and a behavior (i.e., latency).

Estimating

At times, accurately counting or timing a specific practice may be next to impossible; the teacher is busy teaching, or you (if you're the observer) are collecting data on more than one practice at the same time. In these situations, you can estimate the frequency or duration of a practice using an estimation procedure that breaks the observation period into intervals; the shorter the interval, the more precise your estimate will be. Researchers may use intervals as short as 10 seconds, whereas many teachers and observers find that 1- or 2-minute intervals are sufficient to provide an estimate of how often (or for how long) a practice is implemented. A practice is recorded as occurring during an interval if the practice happened at any time during the interval (i.e., partial-interval recording), if the practice occurred throughout the entire interval (i.e., whole-interval recording), or if the practice occurred at the moment the interval ends (i.e., momentary time sampling). In general, partial-interval recording may overestimate the occurrence of a practice or behavior, whole-interval recording may underestimate the occurrence of a practice or behavior, and momentary time sampling falls between the two (but is still not as precise as event or duration–latency recording). For many teachers and observers, momentary time sampling is the most efficient procedure because the teacher or observer does not need to pay attention to the occurrence of the practice during the entire interval. The observer can watch and record other specific instructional or behavioral practices during the interval and then, in the moment that the interval ends, simply record the presence or absence of the target CWPBIS practice.

Here's an applied example to illustrate how these estimation procedures work. Miguel, a school behavior coach, has 20 minutes to observe students' independent work time in Ms. Lowe's classroom. Miguel is interested in estimating how much of the time Ms. Lowe spends actively supervising her students (e.g., moving, scanning, interacting). First, Miguel breaks the observation into 20 one-minute intervals. Ms. Lowe began actively supervising 45 seconds into the first interval and continued for the first 10 seconds of the second interval.

- If he is using partial-interval recording, Miguel will record a "+" (or "yes") for both intervals, or 100% of intervals observed.
- If he is using whole-interval recording, Miguel will record a "−" (or "no") for both intervals, or 0% of intervals observed.
- If he is using momentary time sampling, Miguel will record a "yes" for interval 1 (because the active supervision was occurring at the moment the interval ended) and a "no" for interval 2, as the active supervision stopped before the end of that interval; this would yield an estimate of 50% of intervals observed.

Of course, you would never use only two intervals to determine an estimate of the rate or duration of a teacher's implementation of a CWPBIS practice, but we wanted to provide you with examples of what these estimation processes look like and the kind of data they yield.

SELECTING AN APPROPRIATE TOOL AND DEVELOPING A DATA COLLECTION SYSTEM

Now that you've read about a variety of tools that can be used to collect data on teachers' implementation of CWPBIS practices, we turn our discussion to selecting an appropriate tool for your school or district needs. With any data collection process, the goals are, first, to collect data that answer important questions and, second, not to collect more data than you will need or use. In addition, sharing data regularly helps to build trust with teachers and secure their investment in the CWPBIS implementation process; after all, collecting and sharing data demonstrates your commitment to helping them improve their practices. In general, you should have two types of data to begin the data-based decision-making process: implementation fidelity data and data related to student outcomes. Clarifying the exact outcomes you need to measure will guide your selection of an appropriate tool. Below, we describe specific guidelines for collecting implementation fidelity and student outcome data and discuss additional considerations when selecting a tool and developing an effective and efficient data collection system.

Guidelines for Selecting an Implementation Fidelity Measure

In terms of supporting teachers' implementation of CWPBIS practice, measuring implementation fidelity means you need to know whether teachers are implementing CWPBIS practices accurately (i.e., as designed) and consistently enough to support students in their classrooms. Knowing whether teachers are implementing CWPBIS practices with fidelity is critical to determining the best approach to supporting teachers in your school or district. The leadership team can use implementation fidelity data to identify (1) areas of strength; (2) areas that need improvement; (3) whether the areas that need improvement are related to teachers' acquisition of CWPBIS content knowledge, fluency with CWPBIS practices, maintenance of the skills, or their ability to generalize the knowledge into classroom application; and (4) the amount and content of PD needed based on (1), (2), and (3). Because leadership teams usually want information about the implementation of all CWPBIS practices (rather than one or two target practices), we recommend starting with one of the aforementioned observer or self-assessment checklists that align with the CWPBIS practices to collect this information from every classroom in the building. Therefore, your first step is to determine whether teachers will self-assess or whether outside observers (e.g., peers, coaches, administrators) will collect these fidelity-of-implementation data.

Self-assessment can be a nonthreatening and efficient way to collect information related to CWPBIS practices. Self-assessment data could also remain anonymous when collected for aggregation (although this would render providing individual supports for teachers in need nearly impossible, if this is the only data collection process used). For example, during a faculty meeting, you could ask each teacher to fill out an electronic or paper self-assessment form (without collecting names) and then aggregate that information to obtain a picture of how well teachers see themselves implementing CWPBIS practices. Anonymity may encourage teachers to be more honest in their self-assessments, but it also limits the data's usefulness; the data will help determine an overall level of need in the school but will not identify small groups or individuals who may need additional levels of support.

If the limitations of self-assessment are too great for the school or district, consider using one of the observer checklists that align with CWPBIS practices. These checklists can be completed by peers, coaches, or administrators; using an external observer increases the data's level of validity and reliability, and those data are more appropriate to use for making higher stakes decisions (e.g., those decisions requiring an extensive outlay of resources or that will result in substantive changes to current processes). Keep in mind that some observers may need outside training with the checklist you select, and the length of each observation and the overall time needed to collect these data in all classrooms will vary depending on the checklist used.

Prior to collecting any data (either self-assessment or observer-based), we recommend sharing with teachers exactly how the data will and won't be used. For example, you can assure teachers that these data will be used to identify patterns of strengths and weaknesses across the school to guide the development of PD and coaching supports. If groups of teachers or individuals are struggling with implementing CWPBIS practices, tell them that these data will be used only to develop appropriate supports and will not be included as part of their formal teacher evaluations. Also, communicate how the data will be shared. For example, let teachers know that you intend to share only the aggregate data for the school or grade level; no individual teacher's data will be shared. You will also want to let teachers know that they will see their own data (whether it's self- or observer-collected) to help them inform their own practice. Seeing one's own data is a critical component of performance feedback, which we discuss later in this chapter.

Fidelity-of-implementation data should be collected a minimum of three times per year to guide the development of PD related to CWPBIS and to ensure that teachers are benefiting from CWPBIS training. The data themselves will help you determine how often to collect data. For example, if the data indicated that there was a schoolwide pattern of struggles to implement one, some, or all CWPBIS practices, you would collect data more frequently as you revisit your training and prompting processes. Similarly, if your fidelity-of-implementation data indicated that some teachers (i.e., those requiring Tier 2 supports) or a few teachers (i.e., those requiring Tier 3 supports) had greater levels of support needs, you would increase the frequency of your data collection. (If you're wondering what tiered levels of support for teachers would look like, we provide some guidance in Chapter 8.)

Guidelines for Selecting a Student Outcome Measure

Once you have information about the level of fidelity with which teachers are implementing CWPBIS practices in your school or district, the next step is to consider how well students are responding to these practices. Though this book focuses on supporting teachers, our ultimate goal is improving the social, behavioral, and academic outcomes for students, so it's imperative to determine whether our CWPBIS efforts are having a positive impact on students. We recommend collecting or reviewing student outcome data at least monthly as part of your overall PBIS implementation and using these data (along with your fidelity-of-implementation data) at least three times per year to guide your decision-making processes. It is beyond the scope of this chapter to review all the ways you might measure student outcomes (see Simonsen & Myers, 2015, if you would like a more thorough refresher). Below, we review three measures with particular relevance for supporting teachers' implementation of CWPBIS practices: ODRs, direct ratings of student behavior, and direct observation of student behavior.

Office Discipline Referrals

One common and efficient way to collect information about students' classroom behavior is to review classroom-generated ODRs. ODR data are regularly collected in most schools, making them readily available for review. Data from classroom-generated ODRs provide information about the times of day (e.g., math block, afternoons) associated with higher rates of behaviors that don't meet expectations, which behaviors occur most frequently in classrooms, which grade levels report more challenging behaviors than others, and which specific classrooms have the highest (or lowest) rates of ODRs. Information from ODRs can provide an overview of the prevalence of students' challenging behaviors in some or all classrooms in your school or district. When reviewing ODR data, keep the following considerations (or limitations) in mind. Some inappropriate classroom behaviors may not result in an ODR but instead are handled directly by the classroom teacher, giving you incomplete information about the frequency of inappropriate behaviors and revealing inconsistent responses to inappropriate behaviors across classrooms (and thus the data do not reliably measure the success of CWPBIS implementation across the school). Similarly, minor problem behaviors are not always included in the schoolwide ODR collection but are still a consideration when looking at the success of CWPBIS implementation.

Direct Behavior Ratings

Direct behavior ratings are another option for examining student behavior and may be more accurate and sensitive to change than ODR data. For example, the Direct Behavior Rating measure (DBR; *https://dbr.education.uconn.edu/*) is a quick (i.e., single item per behavior) rating scale with established psychometric proprieties (e.g., Chafouleas, Sanetti, Kilgus, & Maggin, 2012). Teachers can access online training materials to support their use of the DBR. Although initially designed to rate the behavior of an individual student, the DBR can be adapted to collect data on a small group of students or an entire class. The DBR is efficient and can be used repeatedly, making it an option for ongoing progress monitoring. A teacher could complete a self-assessment of CWPBIS implementation and a whole-class DBR at the same time, then compare the results to look for connections and patterns. Collecting DBR data from each classroom in your school could provide information about the overall occurrence of inappropriate classroom behavior, which could then be broken down to provide information about which specific grade levels, groups of teachers, or individuals are reporting the most severe and persistent behavior concerns.

Direct Observation Measures

You may prefer the precision of direct observation measures when collecting data on student behavior in the classroom. If so, and if you have the resources available to conduct direct observation measures on a large enough scale to provide relevant data about school and district CWPBIS implementation, we recommend beginning with an operational definition of the target student behavior (e.g., academically engaged, disruptive) and then selecting a systematic direct observation measurement procedure (many of which are described above) that aligns with the specific target behavior you are observing. For example, you might consider using momentary time sampling to estimate the percentage of observed intervals with academically engaged behavior, or you may use a frequency count to measure the number of times students engaged in disruptive behavior (e.g., talked out) during a lesson. If you are already using direct observation measures to collect data on teachers' use of CWPBIS practices, adding a direct observation measure of student behavior may be an efficient way to collect student outcome data—you'll have the option of targeting one or more specific student behaviors in which you, your teachers, or your staff are particularly interested.

Additional Guidelines for Selecting an Appropriate Tool

We recommend the following guidelines when selecting a measurement tool. First, clearly define the question you are trying to answer. Do you want information on teachers' overall use of CWPBIS practices, or on a specific practice? Which aspect or dimension (e.g., frequency, duration) of the practice is most important for you to capture? These questions will help guide you toward the most appropriate type of measure.

Second, consider the teachers' phase of learning. We described each phase of learning in detail in Chapter 1. Understanding where (in terms of the phases of learning) a teacher is with CWPBIS implementation can help you determine an appropriate measure and data collection process. Are teachers just learning to do the skill accurately (i.e., acquisition)? Are they working to increase the rate at which they use each practice (i.e., fluency)? Are they working to sustain use of the skill over time (i.e., maintenance) or working to adapt their use of the practice to new settings or contexts (i.e., generalization)? For example, if you want to know whether a teacher can use a practice accurately (i.e., the teacher has acquired the skill), one of the observer checklists would be sufficient. However, if you want to know whether the teacher is using a particular practice at an appropriate rate (i.e., the teacher is fluent with the skill), you'll need to use an event-based (e.g., count) or estimation (e.g., partial interval recording) procedure. Collecting data over time (especially in the months and years after CWPBIS training) will help you determine whether teachers are able to maintain their use of a practice. Collecting data across different times of day and across different settings will help you determine whether teachers are able to generalize their use of CWPBIS practices.

Third, consider resources available for collecting data. Do you have staff members who are trained and ready to collect data? Do you have time and money available to support a more rigorous data collection effort using direct observation measures, or will you need to rely on teacher self-assessment and self-report? Having data to guide decision making is essential to effectively and efficiently supporting teachers' CWPBIS implementation, but (as we have mentioned more than once!) there are ways to collect data that use limited resources and still provide you with a strong sense of how the implementation is going. You may sacrifice some accuracy or precision for the sake of efficiency, but, in most cases, self-reported data are sufficient to get started and make decisions about how you can best support CWPBIS implementation moving forward.

Fourth, consider contextual fit. How might the climate and culture of your school and your teachers' comfort with data-based decision making impact the data collection process? In some schools, teachers are used to having observers come in on a regular basis and are comfortable with (and maybe even excited about) having their implementation of CWPBIS practices evaluated. In other schools, an observer in the classroom may cause significant pushback and stress, potentially deterring teachers from engaging in the process. If your school fits into the second category, consider using self-assessments (maybe even anonymously) or having teachers select a peer to observe their implementation of CWPBIS practices. Allow teachers to self-select the areas in which they'd like to improve and demonstrate for teachers how data are used to develop support, not punish. Remember, the purpose of data collection is to build an effective and efficient system of support for teachers. Teachers must be comfortable with the data collection process and trust that the data will be used to support their CWPBIS implementation efforts and the overarching goal of all schools: improving student outcomes.

Finally, consider equity. Specifically, think about equity of access and equity of outcomes. When considering equity of access, ask the following: (1) Do all teachers have equitable access to PD and data collection opportunities? (2) Is your data collection system set up to capture a true picture of teachers' CWPBIS practice use across general education, special education, electives, specials, and both small- and large-group instruction? (3) Does each group of teachers receive equitable access to the training and communication related to your data collection process? When considering equity of outcomes, ask: Are all teachers in your building able to meet the same outcome (e.g., implementing CWPBIS practices with fidelity, increasing the use of specific praise)? Remember, some teachers will need very little support to meet your established outcomes, whereas others will need more. In the next chapter, we discuss differentiated supports and the application of a multi-tiered system of support (MTSS) for teachers.

Putting It All Together

You've now selected multiple assessment measures for multiple variables related to CWPBIS implementation. You're working on assessing teachers' rate of specific CWPBIS practices with an appropriate observation tool and teachers are self-assessing their own implementation. You're assessing fidelity of implementation and monitoring student outcomes. Before determining how best to share these data with teachers, consider how all of these assessment measures work together to "paint a picture" of CWPBIS implementation. How do the data work together to tell the story, and how will you use those data to make decisions? For instance, suppose that our teachers struggle to implement practices. We would immediately look to our fidelity-of-implementation data to ensure that our training had been successful and whether there were other contextual factors to consider. Or, if all CWPBIS practices have been trained and implemented with fidelity but there are no subsequent changes in student outcomes, what else would we need to know? Should we look at other issues related to school climate, additional changes to the curriculum, or personnel shifts? Are our measures reliable and valid? We may need to come up with an overall assessment plan and determine (1) which data are collected when and (2) how those data work together to demonstrate the impact of CWPBIS.

USING DATA TO SUPPORT TEACHERS' IMPLEMENTATION OF CWPBIS PRACTICES

Of course, collecting data using an appropriate tool is only the first step of this process. Those collected data are used to guide the development of efficient and effective supports for teachers as they implement CWPBIS practices. In the next sections, we share guidelines for summarizing and sharing data and using data to provide performance feedback to teachers.

Summarizing Data

Now that you have selected an appropriate tool or tools and have collected your data, what do you do with those data? The first step in efficient, effective use of data is summarizing the data in a format that facilitates decision making rather than just addressing the scope or magnitude of the problem. (Think of the stories you see in the news, many of which are based on newly released data—"Drought now the worst in 100 years!" "Rate of childhood obesity continues to rise!"—but have little to offer in the way of solutions or ideas for changing the current trajectory.) One of the best ways to use data to facilitate decision making is to use visual summaries or graphs of the data you've collected. Graphing data prompts decision making by clarifying trends and facilitating comparisons across categories.

We've found two types of graphs to be most useful when summarizing CWPBIS data. Line graphs help for summarizing data across time, such as a teacher's rate of OTRs across 5 days (Figure 7.1). Bar graphs can also summarize data across time, such as the schools' average CMOT score for each month (Figure 7.2). You could also use a bar graph to compare data across categories, for example, the schools' average CMOT scores by item (Figure 7.3).

Apply the following guidelines when creating and presenting graphs. First, keep graphs simple and follow standard graphing conventions (see Simonsen & Myers, 2015, Chapter 4, for a more detailed discussion of graphing conventions), which help ensure that data are presented and interpreted clearly. Second, use professional graphing programs or applications to generate professional graphs. Third, remember to protect teacher confidentiality when presenting data to more than one teacher (i.e., remove names and aggregate data to avoid singling out any teacher).

Providing Data-Based Performance Feedback

As we described in Chapter 4, effective PD includes (1) training (described in Chapter 5), (2) coaching (described in Chapter 6), and (3) performance feedback (which we're going to describe right now). Generally speaking, **performance feedback** occurs any time you give

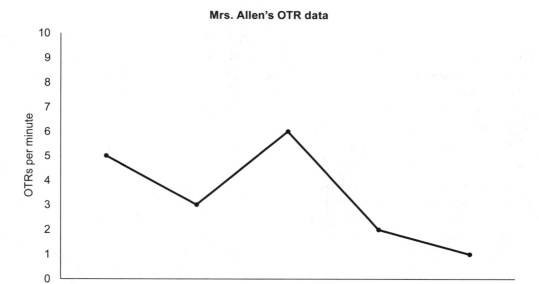

FIGURE 7.1. Line graph example (teacher OTRs).

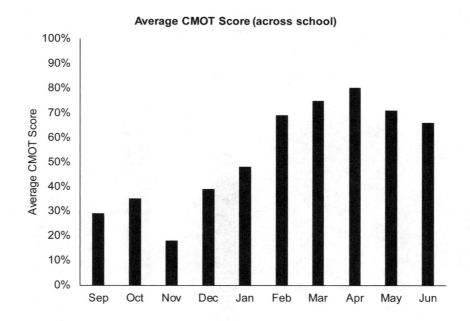

FIGURE 7.2. Bar graph example (CMOT scores across school over time).

someone specific feedback about their behavior. If you're thinking that sounds like specific praise and specific error corrections, you're right! Both specific praise and specific error correction are great examples of performance feedback. However, performance feedback has an added component of sharing data, typically in a line graph, to show trends in behavior across time (e.g., Noell et al., 1997). To support teachers' implementation of CWPBIS practices, the two data sources that may be most critical are levels of CWPBIS implementation (i.e., teacher behavior) and student outcomes (i.e., student behavior).

As we described in the last chapter, we see coaching and performance feedback as functions (not form). So, we believe that teachers or observers (e.g., peers, mentors, coaches, administrators) can effectively collect data, summarize data, and deliver performance feedback for themselves or others. For example, in some of the studies we've conducted (e.g., Simonsen et al., 2017), teachers have (1) collected their own data with a golf counter (one of the methods recommended earlier in this chapter), (2) graphed their own data in a spreadsheet, (3) entered (in the same spreadsheet) quick direct behavior ratings of academically engaged and disruptive behavior in their classrooms, (4) self-evaluated whether their performance met a predetermined goal, and (5) self-reinforced when they met their goal. In other words, teachers effectively engaged in all of the elements of performance feedback for themselves. Figure 7.4 presents an example of a spreadsheet, which we developed to facilitate teachers' self-monitoring and self-delivered performance feedback.

If your school culture and resources support observer-collected performance feedback, you could consider asking observers to collect data and deliver performance feedback. Of course, delivering feedback to someone else is a social skill that can take time and practice

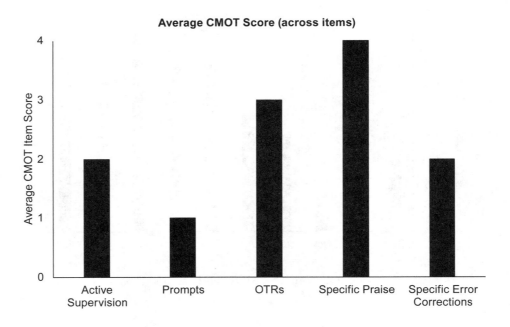

FIGURE 7.3. Bar graph example (CMOT scores across specific CWPBIS practices).

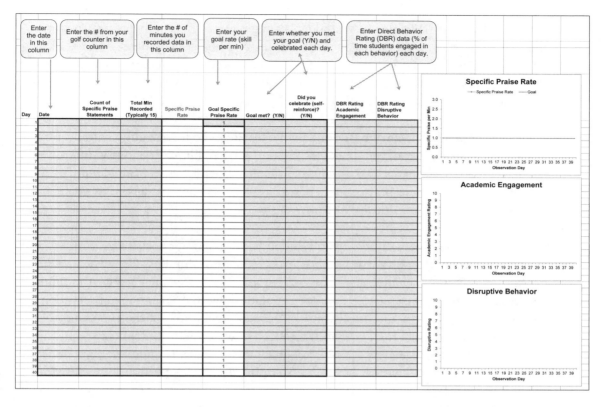

FIGURE 7.4. Example of a spreadsheet to facilitate (1) self-monitoring of specific praise rates, (2) direct behavior rating of students' academically engaged and disruptive behavior, and (3) self-delivered performance feedback (self-evaluation relative to goal and self-reinforcement).

to master. If you're in the early phases of learning to deliver feedback (or are providing training or coaching to others on how to deliver feedback), revisit our discussion on specific praise and specific error corrections. Your performance feedback should be specific, objective, observable, and measurable. If the feedback is corrective in nature, you should deliver it in private using a calm, neutral, or supportive tone and ensure that the feedback is aimed at supporting improvement (rather than punishing current performance).

Imagine, for example, that you are mentoring or coaching another teacher in his or her use of specific praise. You may be working with one teacher who is engaging in desired rates of specific praise and seeing a concurrent improvement in her students' outcomes. In that case, you may share the teacher's graph, highlight a few strong examples of specific praise you observed (yes, you praise her praise!), and celebrate her current rates of praise. For example, you may say (as you show graphs from your observations during the previous week):

"I'm excited to show you these graphs! You've been doing great with praise—you thanked students for raising their hands, you acknowledged correct academic responses, and you provided specific feedback to students engaging in respectful behavior. You'll see that you've been praising consistently—an average of once per minute—during all of my observations for the last week, and your students were academically engaged at least 80% of the time and disruptive less than 20% of the time. Your efforts to increase your specific praise rate are clearly paying off!"

On the other hand, you may be working with a teacher who is struggling with his rates of specific praise. In that case, you'd take a similar approach, but with one key difference: Instead of celebrating successes, you'd want to problem-solve any barriers and identify supports to increase his specific praise rates. For example, you may say (again, as you show graphs from your observations during the previous week):

"Thank you for meeting with me. I can tell that you're making efforts to be positive, as you're using general praise at least once every couple of minutes. However, *specific* praise is presenting a challenge—your current rate is 0.25, or once every 4 minutes, and your goal is to praise once a minute. The data show that during my observations, your students were engaging in disruptive behavior about 40% of the time, and they seem to be engaged less than 60% of the time—so we should think about some ways to improve those outcomes. Let's talk about some strategies to increase your praise. First, you can work to increase how often you give students opportunities to respond, as each time they respond is also an opportunity for you to praise their hand raising, responses—if correct—and their engagement. Second, you may want to script out some specific praise statements you could see yourself using—for example, 'Thank you for raising your hand'—and post reminders for yourself to use those, such as a sticky note in your instructional materials. Third, you could monitor with a golf counter how often you're using praise during 15- or 20-minute periods each day. Which of those strategies sounds like something you want to try? How can I help? I know how hard it is to change our own habits—ask me about the last time I tried to start running—so let's work on this together!"

Remember, delivering error corrections can be challenging, but keeping your focus on the data and on potential solutions will help you remain objective, supportive, and accessible. As we like to say, data don't lie! As soon as you begin to see improvement in a teacher's implementation of CWPBIS practices, be sure to share those data and celebrate success.

Regardless of the specific approach your school or district adopts to implement performance feedback, teachers must receive specific data-based feedback to maintain or enhance their implementation of CWPBIS practices. After all, if you're going to invest the resources and effort to establish CWPBIS, don't you want to make sure that the actual implementers have feedback about how they're doing? Imagine if you helped students prepare for a test, administered the test, and then didn't tell students how they performed on the test (i.e., where they were successful and where they were not successful). Not only would that frustrate a lot of students, but it also wouldn't help them improve their scores for the next assessment. Most teachers will welcome the chance to review their data, learn about their performance, celebrate what is working, and tweak what may need improvement. That's what educators do!

SUMMARY

Supporting teachers' implementation of CWPBIS practices requires the thoughtful collection and use of data to guide decision making. In this chapter, we provided an overview of data collection measures that align with CWPBIS practices, then provided guidelines for selecting appropriate measures for both implementation fidelity and student outcomes. We also discussed how to present data-based feedback to teachers, including examples of feedback for teachers who are meeting their CWPBIS goals and for those who may require additional support. Speaking of additional support, we look at how an MTSS model can be used to support teachers' CWPBIS implementation in the next, and final, chapter.

PHASES OF LEARNING ACTIVITIES: CHAPTER 7

Acquisition

1. Create a list of three data collection tools that may be useful in your school or district and provide your rationale for including each tool on the list. For each tool, identify the primary purpose or best use of the tool and who may be an appropriate person to collect the data.

2. For each of your primary outcome areas (i.e., implementation fidelity and student outcomes), sketch a sample graph of data useful for addressing the key questions.

Fluency

1. Design a presentation (e.g., PowerPoint) describing one or more of the tools you identified in the first "Acquisition" question above. Include a description of what the tool measures, how the data could be collected, and why the tool best fits the needs and context of your school. Include sample data summaries you would develop from the tool to guide decision making.

2. With a colleague, administrator, or coach, practice selecting a tool described in this chapter and "quiz" each other on the guidelines for using each type of tool to check your understanding. Provide a rationale for why you selected the tool and how you will use the data collected with the tool.

Maintenance

1. Visit *www.pbis.org* and review the scenarios in the classroom systems and data guides. Do a check of your own understanding of using data to support CWPBIS, and identify other areas you'd like to explore further.

2. Consider a classroom management training that you have led or attended. Develop a plan to measure the effectiveness of that training. What tools would you choose? Why? What schedule

and process would you use to collect the data? Why? How would you summarize the data? Why?

Generalization

1. Review the content presented in this chapter, then describe any relevant considerations you think would apply when collecting data to guide decision making in the following settings: (1) a small preschool inclusion program, (2) an alternative school or a juvenile justice facility, and (3) a large high school with little existing communication or trust between faculty or across departments.

2. Think about a classroom you are supporting. Develop a plan (based on sample data) to provide performance feedback to the teacher to maintain or enhance implementation of CWPBIS practices. Practice delivering performance feedback with a colleague.

CHAPTER 8

Differentiated Supports for Teachers

CHAPTER OBJECTIVES

By the end of this chapter, you should be able to . . .

1. Use data to answer key questions and differentiate support for CWPBIS implementation as needed at the schoolwide, grade or small-group, classroom, and individual teacher levels.

2. Synthesize and apply all you've learned in the previous chapters to create an effective, efficient, and engaging CWPBIS PD system (including an MTSS to meet the needs of all teachers) for your school or district.

3. Begin thinking ahead to next steps, which could include scaling up implementation (e.g., implementing CWPBIS across an entire district, region, or state) and using implementation-related data to shape school, district, and state policies.

Imagine This: You've been using this book to guide your support of teachers' CWPBIS implementation, and your data indicate that, overall, most teachers are implementing CWPBIS with fidelity. In addition, your data on student outcomes show increases in on-task behavior and decreases in ODRs. However, you do have some teachers who seem to be struggling. Data indicate that these teachers have yet to meet their CWPBIS implementation goals, and students in their classrooms seem to be having more discipline issues than expected. You review your own training and feedback, determine that you've provided these teachers with the same implementation support as the others, and realize that you'll need to increase the frequency and intensity of support for these teachers. You've noticed that throughout this book we've referred to an "MTSS" and "tiered support" for teachers, so you turn to this chapter to get some help.

In Chapter 7, we discussed selecting appropriate tools to collect data on teachers' fidelity of CWPBIS implementation and student outcomes. We also provided an overview of types of data that could be collected and how to represent those data visually (i.e., in graphs). We closed the chapter with a discussion of how those data could be used to provide performance feedback to teachers and emphasized that performance feedback is a critical part of any PD endeavor. In this chapter, we want to take a closer look at the data-based decision-making process and how we can (1) use data to identify teachers who require additional support, (2) create a framework for delivering those differentiated levels of support, and (3) select appropriate supports at each level (or "tier") of support within that framework (i.e., an MTSS).

KEY QUESTIONS TO GUIDE DECISION MAKING

When you have collected all of your data related to CWPBIS implementation, what will you do with them? In Chapter 7, we discussed how those data can be used to provide performance feedback to teachers and increase the likelihood of their implementation of CWPBIS practices. Below, we revisit the data-based decision-making process that we introduced in Chapter 3 and organized graphically in Figure 3.1 and the explanation of data collection in the previous chapter. If you haven't read them recently, we suggest a quick review of Chapters 3 and 7 before you dive too deeply into this chapter.

The data-based decision-making process begins by examining implementation fidelity of CWPBIS practices. Ask: **Are all teachers implementing CWPBIS practices accurately?** If the answer is "yes," celebrate with your staff and continue to monitor implementation fidelity across time to ensure that teachers are maintaining and generalizing their use of CWPBIS practices. See Figure 8.1 for an overview of what decision making related to implementation fidelity looks like.

Sometimes the answer to this question will be "no." Although some teachers will be successfully implementing all CWPBIS practices, others likely will not. Rather than immediately looking for ways to support each teacher individually, consider developing a more efficient plan. Start by using your data to ask: **How many or what percentage of teachers are not yet implementing all CWPBIS practices accurately?** If the answer to this is "many teachers" (e.g., 75–80%), we recommend that you revisit your PD plan and intensify the universal level of CWPBIS-related PD supports (i.e., Tier 1) you've already offered to all teachers. For example, you might consider providing a booster session to review the basic CWPBIS practices, intensifying coaching supports to model CWPBIS practices, or increasing the frequency of performance feedback to help teachers apply their knowledge to their specific classroom contexts.

If the answer to this question is "only a few teachers" (e.g., fewer than 20%), **determine the type and severity of the implementation challenges**. Are teachers struggling with just one or two practices, or are they encountering more severe implementation challenges across multiple aspects of CWPBIS? If teachers are struggling with one or two practices or are able to implement each practice accurately but not in a way that is contextually appropriate for their instructional setting, you could plan to provide supplemental supports (i.e., Tier 2) for this small group of teachers. For example, you might organize a small professional learning community (in which members observe each other, collect data, provide feedback

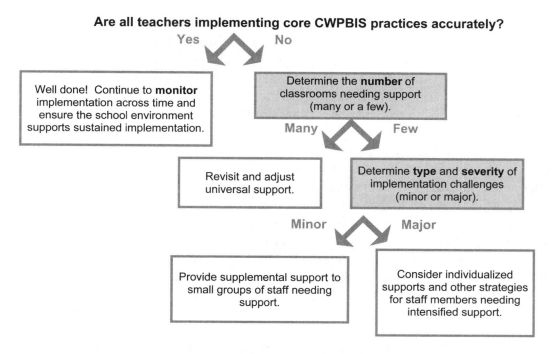

FIGURE 8.1. Implementation fidelity flow chart. From Freeman et al. (2017).

to each other, and share successes and challenges) or set up peer coaching supports focused on the particular implementation challenges faced by this group of teachers.

If you have only one or two teachers encountering more severe implementation challenges, consider more intensive individualized supports (i.e., Tier 3) for these teachers (e.g., frequent, individualized consultation and performance feedback). This level of support may be resource-intensive, but if you've done well implementing universal and supplemental supports, the overall number and severity of implementation challenges will likely be reduced, and you'll have additional resources to use with those teachers who need more intensive support. In the next section, we look more closely at developing a framework for providing teachers with multiple tiers of support related to CWPBIS implementation.

Once you have systems in place to ensure that most teachers are implementing CWPBIS practices accurately, **determine whether student outcomes indicate that these practices are implemented effectively** (e.g., at an appropriate rate and with sufficient intensity). We discussed ways to collect and evaluate data on student outcomes in Chapter 7. If data on student outcomes indicate that CWPBIS practices are being implemented with fidelity, celebrate with your staff (again!) and continue to monitor both implementation fidelity and student outcomes so you can intervene quickly and proactively to address any concerns that arise. If all students are not yet responding to the level and intensity of CWPBIS strategies provided in classrooms, we recommend asking some additional questions to develop a precise picture of the problem.

Specifically, use your data to determine **who** (i.e., which students), **what** (i.e., which behaviors), **where** (i.e., in what parts of the school or classroom or during which school or classroom routines), and **why** (i.e., what is the hypothesized function of the problem behaviors). You may need to collect additional student outcome data in order to address each of these questions. For example, a review of your general schoolwide data indicates that not all students are responding to the current level of CWPBIS practices, and you decide to take a closer look. You examine specific aspects of your ODR data and determine that most of the problem behaviors in classrooms (1) involved fifth-grade students, (2) were related to disrespect or defiance, and (3) were primarily occurring right after lunch. You hypothesize that this group of fifth-grade students is engaging in disrespectful behaviors after lunch in order to obtain peer attention (i.e., they want to maintain "lunch levels" of peer attention after returning to class). This hypothesis is an example of a **precise problem statement** and leads quickly and easily to the next step of this process: action planning.

Once you have developed a clear and precise understanding of the problem at the school or classroom level, the next step is to develop an action plan. An effective action plan addressing a precise problem statement will include (1) ways to prevent the problem from occurring, (2) ways to teach and recognize appropriate behaviors, (3) removing reinforcement contingent on the problem behavior, and (4) providing corrective feedback for problem behaviors (PBISApps, 2016). Table 8.1 provides an example of an action plan for the group of fifth-graders described above.

The action plan in Table 8.1 is just one example of how to structure the intensification of CWPBIS practice implementation to target a specific need identified through a review of data related to student outcomes. Each action plan requires reviewing your PD and data collection plans to ensure both that teachers have the skills and support they need to successfully implement the action plan and that data indicate that the action plan was implemented with fidelity and that students' behaviors have responded to CWPBIS implementation (i.e., appropriate behaviors have increased and inappropriate behaviors have decreased). If your data indicate that teachers require additional support and skills, you can use the decision-making process described above (i.e., Do all, some, or a few teachers

TABLE 8.1. Sample Action Plan for Increasing Behavioral Supports

Solution component	Action step(s)
Prevention	Plan interactive peer-focused activities as a transition back from lunch and increase active supervision during this time.
Teaching	Teach or reteach social skills related to obtaining peer attention appropriately.
Recognition	Implement a group contingency to recognize students who are engaged in appropriate classroom behavior.
Extinction	Plan to handle any problem behaviors privately to avoid increasing peer attention and awareness.
Corrective consequence	When students engage in disrespectful behavior, quietly correct this behavior and remind them that they can gain the respect of their peers by contributing productively to the class discussion and activity.

need additional support and skills?) and the MTSS framework described below to provide differentiated support for teachers and maximize the success of CWPBIS implementation.

OVERVIEW OF AN MTSS FOR SUPPORTING TEACHERS' CWPBIS IMPLEMENTATION

Throughout this book (and especially in the previous sections of this chapter), we have alluded to the benefits and the necessity of developing an MTSS for teachers. By now, you know that a PBIS framework, like a response-to-intervention framework, is based on providing tiered levels of support. The first level of support is an organized, universal, and preventative system designed to provide support to all members of a group—for example, all students in a school (SWPBIS) or all students in a classroom (CWPBIS). The intensity of support increases with each tier; for example, in a SWPBIS framework, the school leadership team may select Check-In/Check-Out (CICO; Crone, Hawken, & Horner, 2010) as a targeted Tier 2 intervention for students who are at risk for challenging behavior and those students who don't respond to Tier 1 interventions. Students who need more individualized supports may benefit from Tier 3 interventions, which could include functional behavioral assessment and behavioral intervention planning, a referral to special education, and/or a comprehensive wraparound model to meet all of a student's behavioral, social, and academic needs. At each tier, we have specific **outcomes**, and we develop **systems** (which include empirically supported **practices**, such as CWPBIS strategies and effective PD techniques) and collect and evaluate **data** to ensure that we are making adequate progress toward our selected outcomes. We explained these core PBIS features in Chapter 1 and have referenced them throughout the book, so we're hoping you've built fluency with them and can generalize your knowledge about outcomes, systems, data, and practices to your own support of teachers' CWPBIS implementation.

Researchers have proposed that an MTSS is a viable approach for providing PD to teachers (e.g., Simonsen et al., 2014). When developing an MTSS to support teachers' implementation of CWPBIS practices, school and district leadership teams could use the following guidelines to construct their tiers of support:

- Tier 1: PD in evidence-based CWPBIS practices provided to all teachers in a school or district with a documented data collection plan to determine whether each teacher's implementation of CWPBIS is successful.
- Tier 2: Targeted support for teachers who require assistance with implementing CWPBIS practices with fidelity (e.g., self-management, professional learning communities).
- Tier 3: Individualized supports for those teachers who require more intensive assistance with implementing CWPBIS practices with fidelity (e.g., frequent, data-driven consultation).

In Table 8.2, we share examples of what the supports can look like at each tier of an MTSS for teachers who are implementing CWPBIS.

TABLE 8.2. Examples of MTSS Supports for Teachers Implementing CWPBIS

Tier	Examples of supports provided	Common features of each tier
Universal (professional development provided to all teachers and staff in a school)	• Explicit training in CWPBIS practices. • Access to coaching supports as needed. • Performance feedback and access to evaluative data to assess CWPBIS implementation.	Ongoing progress monitoring (e.g., reviewing fidelity-of-implementation data; analyzing student outcome data).
Targeted (provided to small groups of teachers requiring additional support with CWPBIS implementation)	• Professional learning communities formed specifically to provide additional supports (e.g., teachers can observe each other and provide feedback on CWPBIS practice implementation). • Coaching supports may be focused on developing teachers' self-management skills so teachers can monitor their own implementation of CWPBIS practices and determine whether they are implementing with fidelity and meeting performance goals.	Using data from progress monitoring to increase or decrease level of support provided to teachers. Celebrating successes.
Individualized (provided to those teachers who have more serious implementation challenges)	• One-on-one consultation with behavior coach; meetings include review of data, goal setting, and modeling of CWPBIS practices. • Increased prompting (e.g., daily emails, sticky notes) to increase likelihood of CWPBIS practice implementation.	

You may notice that our suggestions for Tier 2 and Tier 3 supports are not markedly different from those supports we recommend for Tier 1 CWPBIS implementation, and you may also notice that these supports overlap. This is by design, not by accident. When you're providing a Tier 1 (i.e., universal) level of support to teachers implementing CWPBIS, you're giving clear instructions through your training, providing coaching and prompting, and delivering performance feedback, all while collecting data to support those processes. If you have a group, a few, or one or two teachers who are struggling to implement one or several CWPBIS practices, you will use what you already know about training, coaching, and providing performance feedback to help support those teachers. How you provide those supports may look different across the tiers; for example, you may provide more intensive coaching supports to a grade-level team whose student outcomes have shown an increase in ODRs and provide a booster training in specific CWPBIS practices where the teachers have an identified need. If you have one teacher who simply cannot master specific error correction, you will use what you already know about modeling practices and demonstrate that skill, and you will provide consultation and performance feedback (just as you would for teachers receiving Tier 1 and Tier 2 levels of support), but the schedule of consultation and feedback will likely be more intense. For example, you may review all teachers' data and share those data with all teachers (in aggregate form) on a monthly basis, you may review some teachers' data and share those data with those teachers (in aggregate form) on a weekly basis (i.e., Tier 2), and you may review a few teachers' data and share those data with those teachers (in individualized form) on a daily basis. More intensive coaching and prompting can be done at the small-group or individual-teacher level, as well. You'll use what you already know about supporting adult behavior and adjust the intensity and frequency of those supports in accordance with your teachers' needs.

We'd like you to remember something else about differentiated support. Tier 2 and Tier 3 supports (in any MTSS) are not intended to be in place permanently; they are designed to address areas of need efficiently and effectively. Hopefully, your ongoing data collection and evaluation will indicate that your teachers have begun to implement CWPBIS practices with fidelity and are meeting their goals for implementation (and that student outcome data indicate improvement in teachers' CWPBIS practice implementation). Once you and your team have enough evidence to determine that teachers are able to maintain and generalize their successful implementation of CWPBIS practices, you can begin to fade supports. When you are establishing supports for small groups and individual teachers, be sure to determine some **decision rules** for when those supports will be faded. That is, how long (e.g., across how many observations, how many days, how many weeks) will you need to see sustained improvement (i.e., teachers meeting their performance goals) before you (and the teachers) are confident that successful CWPBIS implementation can be maintained? The performance goals and the criteria for success (and evidence of maintenance) will be based on contextual factors, as well as individual teacher factors (e.g., Is this just one area in which a teacher is struggling to meet expectations, or is there a pattern across PD initiatives?). You can begin by determining what constitutes a need for Tier 2 and Tier 3 support and then use those same decision rules to fade supports as teachers' implementation improves. For example, if teachers who have higher-than-average rates of ODRs are usually provided with Tier 2 supports, then, when those teachers' classroom ODRs are reduced to average (or hopefully below average), Tier 2 supports can begin to be faded (e.g., provided less frequently). Similarly, if teachers who average fewer than one specific praise statement every 3 minutes are usually provided with Tier 3 supports, then, when those teachers' specific praise rates exceed an average of one statement every 3 minutes, you may consider beginning to fade Tier 3 supports (while moving toward Tier 2 supports). Whatever you and your team determine for your decision rules, be sure you don't fade supports too quickly, as this may result in extinction of the newly established behavior of implementing CWPBIS practices with fidelity.

In an MTSS for teachers (as in any tiered system of support), consistent data collection and continuous progress monitoring determine who requires additional support, what those supports will look like, and how those supports will be delivered (and faded as teachers' fidelity of CWPBIS implementation improves). School and district leaders who use an MTSS framework to provide PD in CWPBIS (or when implementing any other school or district initiatives) have a higher likelihood of successful achievement of outcomes than traditional PD models, which often rely on a 1- or 2-day isolated training to produce a lasting impact on teacher behavior.

CONCLUSION

Wrapping Up

We've covered a lot of content in these eight chapters, and we would be remiss if we didn't provide a quick summary before we say goodbye. One last time, we'd like to ask you to . . .

Imagine This: You've just finished your first year leading your school's CWPBIS implementation. All teachers in the school received CWPBIS training at the beginning of the year; throughout the year, you and your team provided coaching, prompting, and feedback to help teachers become fluent with and maintain their CWPBIS practices. You've also provided additional help to teachers who required additional supports to implement CWPBIS with fidelity, including establishing a professional learning community for those who wanted to access additional peer support and providing weekly (and even daily) feedback on teachers' implementation of CWPBIS practices as necessary. Overall, it has been a successful year, and the measures you've used to determine whether your teachers are implementing CWPBIS with fidelity indicate that your efforts have been working. ODRs are down, teachers' implementation of CWPBIS practices is up (according to the CMOT conducted schoolwide in May, which showed marked improvement when compared with baseline data from September), and, anecdotally, morale seems to be improved across the school. As you begin to daydream about your summer vacation, a little voice creeps into your head and whispers, "Now what?"

Looking Back

By now, we hope you've acquired the knowledge and built fluency with the content you need to successfully support teachers' implementation of CWPBIS practices. You've learned about the underlying behavioral principles that are the foundation of CWPBIS practices and adult behavior change. You've learned about PD models and what training, coaching behaviors, prompting, and feedback should look like when supporting teachers. You've learned about the critical role of data when supporting teachers' implementation of CWPBIS practices, and how to use those data to differentiate support (and even build a tiered system of support for teachers). If you've worked through the activities at the end of each chapter, you've developed a number of resources to help you support teachers' implementation of CWPBIS, including glossaries of relevant terms and concepts, timelines and action plans to shape your PD, training materials and presentations you can use, and tools to measure the success of your efforts. In addition, we hope we've prepared you for the challenges and rewards that come with supporting teachers' implementation of CWPBIS practices. As we mentioned back in Chapter 2, changing the likelihood of behaviors in adults is challenging; after all, if we've been behaving a certain way for a long time, we're likely to keep engaging in those behaviors unless there's a *really* good reason for us to change our behavior. Hopefully, the benefits that come with effective CWPBIS implementation (and the additional reinforcers and antecedent strategies, such as prompts and effective training, that you've employed) will bring about the desired change in teachers' behavior.

Looking Ahead

If you've had success in supporting teachers' implementation of CWPBIS, you may be thinking about what comes next. As with other decisions related to providing support, what comes next will depend on the specific context in which you're working. If you've overseen successful implementation of CWPBIS across all classrooms in an elementary school, you may be interested in helping teams at other elementary schools in your district begin the CWPBIS implementation process. You may want to work with the middle school (and eventually the high school) that your students are most likely to attend to provide continuity of behavior supports and adapt what you've learned at the elementary level to middle and high school contexts. If you've overseen successful CWPBIS implementation at a district level, maybe you are interested in looking at how to expand efforts across your region or even your state.

Maybe you're thinking on a slightly smaller scale. For instance, maybe you're just one teacher who has successfully implemented CWPBIS in your classroom, and you want to use what you've learned to help your grade-level colleagues implement CWPBIS in their classrooms. We say, use what you've learned from this book and go for it! The same critical features (e.g., explicit training, coaching, feedback, data collection, ongoing monitoring) still apply. Maybe you've had success with implementing CWPBIS across your school and now you'd like your teachers to be able to implement more intensive (i.e., Tier 2 and Tier 3) supports at the classroom level. To do that, we'd recommend that you review Chapters 9 and 10 in Simonsen and Myers (2015) to see what more intensive supports can look like at the classroom level, and then use what you've learned in this book to move forward with supporting teachers' implementation of those increasingly intensive supports.

Saying Goodbye

Whatever your next steps, it's important that you continue to evaluate and adapt your CWPBIS system as needed. Work toward creating a culture of continuous improvement, in which you and your team regularly review data, identify areas of strength and any areas where improvement is needed, and determine how to provide additional supports, retraining, or follow-up as indicated by the data. We hope you'll turn back to this book often if you need a refresher, and we encourage you to use the tools within (and the others we've suggested) to support *your* support of teachers' implementation of CWPBIS. We're glad you're a part of our PBIS journey, and we wish you the best with your support of teachers' implementation of CWPBIS.

PHASES OF LEARNING ACTIVITIES: CHAPTER 8

Acquisition

1. Create a visual guide (e.g., checklist, graphic organizer) for you and your team that walks you through the data-making decision process. Be sure to include the key questions and the tasks that need to be completed at each stage of the process.

2. Write a hypothetical example of a precise problem statement that describes an issue in your school or district and create an action plan (like the one in Table 8.1) that includes specific details about how you'd increase behavioral supports.

Fluency

1. Design a presentation (e.g., PowerPoint) that you could use to illustrate the data-based decision-making process as related to teachers' implementation of CWPBIS. Include applied, contextually relevant examples for your school or district.

2. Review Table 8.2 and, for each of the "Examples of Supports Provided," write out specific scenarios of what those examples might look like at your school or in your district. Who would be delivering the supports, and who would be receiving them? Where, how, and when would they be delivered?

Maintenance

1. Review your school's or district's fidelity of CWPBIS implementation and related student outcome data, then develop some initial decision rules that you and your team could use to determine when teachers require additional levels of support. These rules could (and should) be related to both fidelity of implementation and student outcome data.

2. We often use a triangle to illustrate MTSSs. We didn't include one in this chapter because we wanted you to develop your own, based on the levels of support you will provide in your school or district. Construct a triangle model (using paper and pencil or a computer, if you have the skills) and indicate the types of supports *and* the characteristics of implementation fidelity (e.g., strong, mostly strong, needs improvement) you'd see at each level.

Generalization

1. Using what you've learned in this book, create an organized handbook (e.g., electronic binder, physical binder) that you and your team can use to guide your support of teachers' CWPBIS implementation in your school or district. Consider structuring your handbook around outcomes, systems, data, and practices and be sure to include action plans, timelines, and all other information (including products from the tasks you've completed as part of each chapter's "Phases of Learning" activities) you would need to successfully support your teachers' implementation of CWPBIS.

2. Reflect on your experiences with supporting teachers' CWPBIS implementation. What have you learned? What has been most exciting? What has presented challenges? What would you replicate if you were to support another school or district, and what might you do differently? Write up your reflection and save it somewhere convenient, so you can revisit it if and when you have the opportunity to participate in supporting a different group of teachers' implementation of CWPBIS in the future.

References

Alberto, P. A., & Troutman, A. C. (2016). *Applied behavior analysis for teachers* (interactive 9th ed.). New York: Pearson.

Algozzine, B., Barrett, S., Eber, L., George, H., Horner, R., Lewis, T., . . . Sugai, G. (2014). *School-wide PBIS Tiered Fidelity Inventory.* Eugene, OR: OSEP Technical Assistance Center on Positive Behavioral Interventions and Supports.

Archer, A. L., & Hughes, C. A. (2011). *Explicit instruction: Effective and efficient teaching.* New York: Guilford Press.

Bijou, S. W., & Baer, D. M. (1961). *Child development: A systematic and empirical theory.* New York: Appleton-Century-Crofts.

Borgmeier, C., Loman, S., & Hara, M. (2016). Teacher self-assessment of evidence-based classroom practices: Preliminary findings across primary-, intermediate-, and secondary-level teachers. *Teacher Development, 20*(1), 40–56.

Brophy, J., & Good, T. (1986). Teacher behavior and student achievement. In M. C. Wittrock (Ed.), *Handbook of research on teaching* (3rd ed., pp. 376–391). New York: Macmillan.

Carr, E. G., Dunlap, G., Horner, R. H., Koegel, R. L., Turnbull, A. P., Sailor, W., . . . Fox, L. (2002). Positive behavior support: Evolution of an applied science. *Journal of Positive Behavior Interventions, 4,* 4–16, 20.

Chafouleas, S. M., Sanetti, L. M. H., Kilgus, S. P., & Maggin, D. M. (2012). Evaluating sensitivity to behavioral change across consultation cases using Direct Behavior Rating Single-Item Scales (DBR-SIS). *Exceptional Children, 78,* 491–505.

Cooper, J. O., Heron, T. E., & Heward, W. L. (2007). *Applied behavior analysis* (2nd ed.). Upper Saddle River, NJ: Prentice Hall.

Crone, D. A., Hawken, L. S., & Horner, R. H. (2010). *Responding to problem behavior in schools: The Behavior Education Program* (2nd ed.). New York: Guilford Press.

Darling-Hammond, L., Hyler, M. E., & Gardner, M. (2017). *Effective teacher professional development.* Palo Alto, CA: Learning Policy Institute.

Dynamic Measurement Group. (2008). *DIBELS 6th Edition Technical Adequacy Information* (Tech. Rep. No. 6). Eugene, OR: Author. Retrieved from *http://dibels.org/pubs.html.*

Fixsen, D. L., Blase, K. A., Duda, M. A., Naoom, S. F., & Van Dyke, M. (2010). Implementation of evidence-based treatments for children and adolescents: Research findings and their implications for the future. In J. R. Weisz & A. E. Kazdin (Eds.), *Evidence-based psychotherapies for children and adolescents* (p. 435–450). New York: Guilford Press.

Fixsen, D., Blase, K., Naoom, S., & Duda, M. (2013). *Implementation drivers: Assessing best practices*. Chapel Hill, NC: National Implementation Research Network. Retrieved from *www.researchgate.net/publication/307967873_Implementation_Drivers_Assessing_Best_Practices*.

Fixsen, D. L., Naoom, S. F., Blase, K. A., Friedman, R. M., & Wallace, F. (2005). *Implementation research: A synthesis of the literature* (FMHI Publication No. 231). Tampa: University of South Florida, Louis de la Parte Florida Mental Health Institute, National Implementation Research Network.

Forman, S. G., Olin, S. S., Eaton Hoagwood, K., Crowe, M., & Saka, N. (2009). Evidence-based interventions in schools: Developers' views of implementation barriers and facilitators. *School Mental Health, 1*, 26–36.

Freeman, J., Simonsen, B., Briere, D. E., & MacSuga-Gage, A. S. (2014). Preservice teacher training in classroom management: A review of state accreditation policy and teacher preparation programs. *Teacher Education and Special Education, 37*, 106–120.

Freeman, J., Simonsen, B., Goodman, S., Mitchell, B., George, H. P., Swain-Bradway, J., . . . Putnam, B. (2017). *PBIS technical brief on systems to support teachers' implementation of positive classroom behavior support*. Eugene, OR: PBIS Center. Retrieved from *www.pbis.org/Common/Cms/files/pbisresources/PBIS%20Technical%20Brief%20on%20Systems%20to%20Support%20Teachers%20Implementation%20of%20Positive%20Classroom%20Behavior%20Support.pdf*.

Freeman, J., Sugai, G., Simonsen, B., & Everett, S. (2017). MTSS coaching: Bridging knowing into doing. *Theory into Practice, 56*, 29–37.

Gresham, F. M., & Elliott, S. N. (2008). *Social Skills Improvement System Rating Scales manual*. Minneapolis, MN: NCS Pearson.

Horner, R. H., & Albin, R. W. (1988). Research on general-case procedures for learners with severe disabilities. *Education and Treatment of Children, 11*(4), 375–388.

Horner, R. H., Vaughn, B., Day, H. M., & Ard, W. R. (1996). The relationship between setting events and problem behavior: Expanding our understanding of behavioral support. In L. K. Koegel & R. L. Koegel (Eds.), *Positive behavioral support: Including people with difficult behavior in the community* (pp. 381–402). Baltimore: Brookes.

IRIS Center. (2010). Fidelity of implementation: Selecting and implementing evidence-based practices and programs. Retrieved from *https://iris.peabody.vanderbilt.edu/module/fid*.

Jeffrey, J. L., McCurdy, B. L., Ewing, S., & Polis, D. (2009). Classwide PBIS for students with EBD: Initial evaluation of an integrity tool. *Education and Treatment of Children, 32*, 537–550.

Joyce, B., & Showers, B. (2002). *Student achievement through staff development* (3rd ed.). Alexandria, VA: ASCD.

Klassen, R. M., & Chiu, M. M. (2010). Effects on teachers' self-efficacy and job satisfaction: Teacher gender, years of experience, and job stress. *Journal of Educational Psychology, 102*, 741–756.

Kraft, M. A., Blazar, D., & Hogan, D. (2018). The effect of teacher coaching on instruction and achievement: A meta-analysis of the causal evidence. *Review of Educational Research, 88*(4), 547–588.

La Salle, T. P., McIntosh, K., & Eliason, B. M. (2018). *School climate survey suite administration manual*. Eugene: University of Oregon, OSEP Technical Assistance Center on Positive Behavioral Interventions and Supports.

Landers, E., Alter, P., & Servilio, K. (2008). Students' challenging behavior and teachers' job satisfaction. *Beyond Behavior, 18*, 27–33.

Laraway, S., Snycerski, S., Michael, J., & Poling, A. (2003). Motivating operations and terms to describe them: Some further refinements. *Journal of Applied Behavior Analysis, 36*, 407–414.

Lever, N., Castle, M., Cammack, N., Bohnenkamp, J., Stephan, S., Bernstein, L., . . . Sharma, R.

(2014). *Resource mapping in schools and school districts: A resource guide.* Baltimore: Center for School Mental Health.

Lewis, T., & Newcomer, L. (2002). Examining the efficacy of school-based consultation: Recommendations for improving outcomes. *Child and Family Behavior Therapy, 24,* 165–181.

May, S., Ard, W., Todd, A., Horner, R., Glasgow, A., Sugai, G., & Sprague, J. (2010). *Schoolwide Information System v4.5.217.* Eugene: University of Oregon.

Missouri Schoolwide Positive Behavior Support. (2018). MO SW-PBS Tier 1 Team Workbook. Retrieved from *http://pbismissouri.org/wp-content/uploads/2018/05/MO-SW-PBS-Tier-1-2018. pdf?x30198.*

Myers, D., Freeman, J., Simonsen, B., & Sugai, G. (2017). Classroom management with exceptional learners. *Teaching Exceptional Children, 49,* 223–230.

Myers, D., Sugai, G., Simonsen, B., & Freeman, J. (2017). Assessing teachers' behavior support skills. *Teacher Education and Special Education, 40,* 128–139.

National Commission on Teaching and America's Workforce. (2016). *What matters now: A new compact for teaching and learning.* Arlington, VA: National Commission on Teaching and America's Future. Retrieved from *www.nysed.gov/common/nysed/files/principal-project-what-matters-now.pdf.*

Noell, G. H., Witt, J. C., Slider, N. J, Connell, J. E., Gatti, S. L., Williams K. L., . . . Duhon, G. J. (2005). Treatment implementation following behavioral consultation in schools: A comparison of three follow-up strategies. *School Psychology Review, 34,* 87–106.

Office of Special Education Programs. (2015). Supporting and responding to behavior: Evidence-based classroom strategies for teachers. Retrieved from *www.osepideasthatwork.org/evidence-basedclassroomstrategies.*

Oliver, R. M., & Reschly, D. J. (2007). *Effective classroom management: Teacher preparation and professional development.* Washington, DC: National Comprehensive Center for Teacher Quality. Retrieved from *www.tqsource.org/topics/effectiveClassroomManagement.pdf.*

Oliver, R. M., & Reschly, D. J. (2010). Special education teacher preparation in classroom management: Implications for students with emotional and behavioral disorders. *Behavioral Disorders, 35,* 188–199.

PBISApps. (2016). SWIS drill-down worksheet. Retrieved from *www.pbisapps.org/Resources/ SWIS%20Publications/SWIS%20Drill%20Down%20Worksheet.docx.*

Pianta, R. C., La Paro, K. M., & Hamre, B. K. (2008). *Classroom Assessment and Scoring System (CLASS): Manual.* Baltimore: Brookes.

Reddy, L. A., Dudek, C. M., Fabiano, G., & Peters, S. (2015). Measuring teacher self-report on classroom practices: Construct validity and reliability of the Classroom Strategies Scale—Teacher Form. *School Psychology Quarterly, 30*(4), 513–533.

Reddy, L. A., Fabiano, G., Dudek, C. M., & Hsu, L. (2013). Development and construct validity of the Classroom Strategies Scale—Observer Form. *School Psychology Quarterly, 28,* 317–341.

Reinke, W. M., Herman, K. C., Stormont, M., Newcomer, L., & David, K. (2013). Illustrating the multiple facets and levels of fidelity of implementation to a teacher classroom management intervention. *Administration and Policy in Mental Health and Mental Health Services Research, 40,* 494–506.

Simonsen, B., Fairbanks, S., Briesch, A., Myers, D., & Sugai, G. (2008). Evidence-based practices in classroom management: Considerations for research to practice. *Education and Treatment of Children, 31,* 351–380.

Simonsen, B., Fairbanks, S., Briesch, A., & Sugai, G. (2006). Classroom management: Self-assessment revised. Retrieved from *http://neswpbs.org/sites/default/files/7r_classroom_management_self-assessment.pdf.*

Simonsen, B., Freeman, J., Dooley, K., Maddock, E., Kern, L., & Myers, D. (2017). Effects of targeted professional development on teachers' specific praise rates. *Journal of Positive Behavior Interventions, 19,* 37–47.

Simonsen, B., Freeman, J., Kooken, J., Dooley, K., Gambino, A. J., Wilkinson, S., . . . Kern, L. (2020). Initial validation of the Classroom Management Observation Tool (CMOT). *School Psychology.*

Simonsen, B., Freeman, J., MacSuga-Gage, A., Briere, D., III, Freeman, J., Myers, D., . . . Sugai, G. (2014). Multitiered support framework for teachers' classroom-management practices: Overview and case study of building the triangle for teachers. *Journal of Positive Behavior Interventions, 16,* 179–190.

Simonsen, B., Freeman, J., Swain-Bradway, J., George, H., Putnam, B., Lane, K., . . . Hersheldt, P. (2019). Using data to support teachers' implementation of empirically supported classroom practices. *Education and Treatment of Children, 42,* 265–290.

Simonsen, B., & Myers, D. (2015). *Classwide positive behavior interventions and supports: A guide to proactive classroom management.* New York: Guilford Press.

Simonsen, B., Myers, D., & DeLuca, C. (2010). Teaching teachers to use prompts, opportunities to respond, and specific praise. *Teacher Education and Special Education, 33,* 300–318.

Skinner, B. F. (1953). *Science and human behavior.* New York: Free Press.

Sprague, J., Colvin, G., & Irvin, L. (2003). *The school safety survey.* Eugene: University of Oregon.

Stokes, T. F., & Baer, D. M. (1977). An implicit technology of generalization. *Journal of Applied Behavior Analysis, 10,* 349–367.

Stumphauzer, J. (1971). A low-cost "bug-in-the-ear" sound system for modification of therapist, parent, and patient behavior. *Behavior Therapy, 2,* 249–250.

Sugai, G., Horner, R. H., Algozzine, R., Barrett, S., Lewis, T., Anderson, C., . . . Simonsen, B. (2010). *Schoolwide positive behavior support: Implementers' blueprint and self-assessment.* Eugene: University of Oregon. Retrieved from *www.pbis.org/implementation/implementers_blueprint. asps.*

Swain-Bradway, J., Putnam, R., Freeman, J., Simonsen, B., George, H. P., Goodman, S., . . . Sprague, J. (2017). *PBIS technical guide on classroom data: Using data to support implementation of positive classroom behavior support practices and systems.* Eugene, OR: National Technical Assistance Center on Positive Behavior Interventions and Support. Retrieved from *www.pbis. org/Common/Cms/files/pbisresources/PCBS%20Data%20Brief%2012.18.17.pdf.*

Turnbull, A., Edmonson, H., Griggs, P., Wickham, D., Sailor, W., Freeman, R., . . . Warren, J. (2002). A blueprint for schoolwide positive behavior support: Implementation of three components. *Exceptional Children, 68,* 377–402.

U.S. Department of Education, Office of Safe and Healthy Students. (2019). *Technical and administration user guide for the ED School Climate Surveys (EDSCLS).* Washington, DC: Author.

Vargas, J. (2013). *Behavior analysis for effective teaching* (2nd ed.). Oxfordshire, UK: Routledge.

Walker, H. M., Horner, R. H., Sugai, G., Bullis, M., Sprague, J., Bricker, D., & Kaufman, M. J. (1996). Integrated approaches to preventing anti-social behavior patterns among school-age children and youth. *Archives of Pediatrics and Adolescent Medicine, 116,* 149–156.

Wallace, F., Blase, K., Fixsen, D., & Naoom, S. (2008). *Implementing the findings of research: Bridging the gap between knowledge and practice.* Alexandria, VA: Educational Research Service.

Yoon, K. S., Duncan, T., Lee, S. W.-Y., Scarloss, B., & Shapley, K. (2007). *Reviewing the evidence on how teacher professional development affects student achievement* (Issues & Answers Report, REL 2007-No. 033). Washington, DC: U.S. Department of Education, Institute of Education Sciences, National Center for Education Evaluation and Regional Assistance, Regional Educational Laboratory Southwest. Retrieved from *http://ies.ed.gov/ncee/edlabs.*

Index

Note. Page numbers in *italic* indicate a figure or a table.